"My friend Taylor Field has been turning the things upside down for years in New York City. He has confounded many who don't think a strong church can be built in such a challenging venue. So much written about leadership is formulaic. Here is a fresh look from a guy who has done it— not some armchair expert but a person who has led and developed leaders in one of the most difficult ministry environments imaginable. Read this book at your risk—it might turn your world upside down."

— DR. JEFF IORG, president, Golden Gate Baptist Theological Seminary and author of *Live Like a Missionary: Giving Your Life for What Matters Most*

"In the 13 years that I have known and have served with Taylor Field, I have seen him lead in some of the most difficult and impossible situations. I have seen him lead a Bible study for a group of homeless men who were only there because they wanted to get out of the cold. I have seen him lead a violent and broken teenager to Christ—and change that kid's life forever. I have seen him lead the building of an incredible church from the ruins of a forgotten neighborhood on the Lower East Side. I have even seen him lead two naive 23-year-old seminary students (me and my wife) to move to New York City and to believe they could actually make a dif- ference here. I am just one of the many lives that has been impacted by Taylor's 'upside-down leadership'!"

— KERRICK THOMAS, coauthor of *Launch: Starting a New Church from Scratch,* pastor of The Journey Church NYC—Upper West and Village campuses,

"I believe this is the only book I've ever read that first captured my atten- tion by the chapter titles! Here is a whole new way to view leadership and it is as refreshing as cool water on a hot, dry day. Taylor Field has the paradoxes of life standing out in sharp view. I discovered gems scattered throughout each chapter and found the 'gallery of unleaders' an amazing source of thoughts and ideas for use in preparing messages. There are some old friends in that gallery and some fresh faces you'll want to know. This is the kind of book you want to keep and refer to repeatedly."

—ROSALIE HALL HUNT, national WMU recording secretary, and author of *Bless God and Take Courage: The Judson History and Legacy*

"In *Upside-Down Leadership: Rethinking Influence and Success*, Taylor Field offers the Christian community a snapshot of what Jesus' words, 'My kingdom is not of this world,' look like in real life. Combining 25 years of experience as a pastor in one of New York City's most challenging neighborhoods with solid biblical interpretation and historical examples, Field offers a needed corrective to the prevailing, secular views on leadership that are too easily and casually embraced in the church. For those of us who know Taylor and his family, they are the embodiment of an 'unleader.' They have followed Jesus to minister to the unglamorous and overlooked in our city. His incarnation of these principles gives this book a compelling ring of authenticity rarely found. Read this book and prepare yourself to be turned upside down!"

—GEORGE T. RUSS, executive director,
Metropolitan New York Baptist Association

"Taylor and Susan Field planted themselves in the Lower East Side at a time that most who could were getting out of the city. Their influence has grown as the result of their efforts repeatedly brought about changed lives. When they began, success could have been measured by conducting an effective ministry center, but their success was magnified by a basic understanding that a strong local church was needed to enhance, preserve, and multiply the impact made upon the lives of individuals whose lives were changed."

—TERRY M. ROBERTSON, executive director/treasurer,
Baptist Convention of New York

"Get compassion, grace, and Christ in your life—and also from this book."

—BRUCE GREER, gospel comedian, unleader,
and best greeter of the homeless, rain or shine

upside
uʍop
LEADERSHIP

RETHINKING INFLUENCE AND SUCCESS

taylor field

NEW HOPE
PUBLISHERS
BIRMINGHAM, ALABAMA

New Hope® Publishers
P. O. Box 12065
Birmingham, AL 35202-2065
www.NewHopeDigital.com
New Hope Publishers is a division of WMU®.

Library of Congress Cataloging-in-Publication Data Library of Congress Cataloging-in-Publication Data

   Field, Taylor.
    Upside-down leadership : rethinking influence and success / Taylor Field.
      p. cm.
    ISBN 978-1-59669-342-5 (sc)
    1. Leadership--Religious aspects--Christianity. I. Title.
    BV4597.53.L43F54 2012
    253--dc23
                              2012003906

Unless otherwise indicated, all Scripture quotations are from The Holy Bible, English Standard Version, copyright © 2001 by Crossway Bibles, a division of Good News Publishers. Used by permission. All rights reserved.

The source of most references in the book can be found at the back of the book under "The Gallery of Unleaders Mentioned in This Book." The names of the people are listed in alphabetical order.

ISBN-10: 1-59669-342-8
ISBN-13: 978-1-59669-342-5

N124147 • 0412 • 3M1

Dedicated to "someone"

"Christianity preaches the infinite worth of that which is seemingly worthless and the infinite worthlessness of that which is seemingly so valued."

Dietrich Bonhoeffer at 22 years old,
giving a lecture to a small group of high schoolers

Acknowledgments

—To Susan, my wife, and to my sons and daughters-in-law, Freeman, Candace, Owen, and Krista, who all remind me that right side up may be upside down.

—To the workers at New Hope Publishers, especially Joyce Dinkins, Andrea Mullins, and Ashley Stephens, for being willing to look at familiar things in order to find the unfamiliar.

—To my fellow travelers at Graffiti, who let me know that what you expect may not be what really is.

Table of Contents

introduction
The Kingdom Is Getting Bigger and Smaller

Those who would take over the earth
And shape it to their will
Never, I notice, succeed.

"The Old Fellow" at the end of his life,
sometime around 6th century B.C. in China

The Upside-Down Man

He had always been an extremely neat and fastidious man, meticulous in his own personal cleanliness. He valued fresh linens and clean shirts, and always insisted on a fresh, black ribbon tie. His books and papers were all neatly ordered and immaculately dusted. Now his head was resting in the human excrement and muck of a prison that was never cleaned. Worst of all, he was upside down. Only his head and a bit of his shoulders touched the ground. They did this to him every night. It was a position designed to make him feel numb without quite killing him. He was with 50 other unwashed prisoners in the dark, all of them nearly naked. They received one five-minute bathroom break every 24 hours. Temperatures exceeded 100 degrees, and the room had no windows and almost no ventilation. The smell alone of the place made you gag. Little could stop the work of a horde of rats and mosquitoes and cockroaches. One of the men close to him had leprosy.

Things look a little different when you are upside down. He could not see much in the dark except the shadows of other humans in pain, hanging just like he was in chains. A long time ago, his mother had taught him that cleanliness was next to godliness. He was taught not to get dirty — what in the world had happened to him? He had been very precocious as a child, and his father was convinced that he would go far in his career. Things hadn't turned out the way his father expected. At one time, as a young man, he had been offered one of the best positions in Boston. It was a position of prestige, where he and his family would be respected for doing good. Grand vistas opened before him then. He had been a great speaker and a scholar with a stellar future. It would have been a good life. That offer was years ago and thousands of miles away. All his current circumstances seemed to spell out a fiasco. I wonder if he had any doubts about his decisions, as he was hanging there in the dark, upside down, hour after hour. I think so.

Things just didn't seem to have turned out as he had hoped. For the first seven years of his time in his job, he did not see any tangible return on all his efforts. And now this. I wonder if he felt waves of self-recrimination because he had put his wife and family into such a brutal situation, alone in a foreign country, in a time of war. We know he was desperately concerned about his wife's safety but totally unable to help her in her danger. I wonder if he felt like a failure as a husband, as a man, and as a scholar. He supposed that all his scholarly work had been totally destroyed when the government ransacked his house. There were hardly any other visible results from his work with the people there, either. The years must have seemed wasted. Some leader he proved to be.

Your point of view depends on your point of viewing, and you can't help but see things differently when you are upside down. You get a better view of failure, the underside of success, and by doing so you see a different view of life than you would otherwise. It's a big kingdom. Adoniram Judson kept affirming to himself that he was a part of that kingdom. Once you get past his first name and the old-time trappings of his calling as a missionary, his difficult life and failed hopes may have something to say to us. In 1834 in a filthy prison in Burma, thousands of miles from where he grew up, the kingdom was getting smaller for Judson—but perhaps bigger at the same time.

Perhaps bigger at the same time. The deprivations for Judson and his pregnant wife and family continued. If you read about their harsh circumstances, they seem endless. Judson survived, but for the rest of his life, he had scars from the chains. The scars weren't the worst part. It would be nice to say that everything worked out for his family. But his wife Ann did not survive, nor did their child who was born when he was in prison.

For me, one of the surprises of growing older was realizing that everything doesn't happen in one generation. No doubt, Adoniram had some very difficult times as a missionary. Reading the stories of his life sometimes seems like there is one ineffective effort and setback after another. Adoniram and Ann Judson are noteworthy; they are considered the first American overseas missionaries. They eventually became well known. But even at the end of Adoniram's life, when he had begun to influence a generation of people, the statistical results of his work in Burma were not huge. It would take many decades and several lifetimes to begin to see the profound influence he has had on Christian growth in the present-day Republic of the Union of Myanmar. We still have not seen the end of his influence. Some things in life are like that, and possibly most of the important things.

The Bee Is Unaware

The tangible results of Adoniram often seemed small or even nonexistent in the country he worked in. Ironically, one of his sons, Edward Judson, ultimately had an extremely successful ministry in Lower Manhattan. The son had a taste for how big the kingdom could be, but perhaps because of his father's experience, he had a sense of a different kind of leadership. Although a scholar, Edward felt drawn to work among immigrants as New York City entered the twentieth century. In Adoniram's first seven years as a missionary, he did not have one convert. In his son Edward's first seven years at the church in Lower Manhattan, 700 people were added to the church. Edward started the first church kindergarten, along with boys and girls clubs. The church provided a gym, training in practical skills, a dispensary, and a children's home. Edward was respected and loved for his leadership. One could see the tangible results of his influence.

On reflecting back, five months before he died Edward spoke about his father to a gathering of Christians and, in a way, Edward spoke about leadership. True, Edward's father and Edward's father's first wife were recognized as the first American missionaries sent overseas. However, Adoniram's son Edward recognized that a sense of failure fell over his father's last years, as his father watched the retrenchment in outreach to others that was so important to him. Yet Edward also saw the profound impact his father was still having in spite of the string of failures and hardships in his life. I find his words worth reading more than once. He said, "We are all the time thinking of what we are doing to our work; God is thinking of what our work is doing to us." What an inversion of the way we normally approach our labors.

Edward said, "The important thing is not to undertake some great piece of work, but to live day by day, having the mind that was in Christ Jesus." Wait a minute. Edward was an effective urban leader. Isn't leadership about undertaking "some great piece of work"? Isn't that the point? Adoniram Judson's son thought about our emphasis on results, but he maintained what many had forgotten, that "large undertakings require more than a lifetime for their fulfillment."

The son of the upside-down man had his own thoughts on our experience of work. We as leaders chase after so many things. But Edward said, "It is the little things that we get by hot chase. The great things come to us, as it were, around a corner, when we are looking for something else." He compares the person to a bee, whose goal is to seek honey, but is really cross-fertilizing a variety of plants. "The best work he is doing, he knows nothing about." How odd to tell a group of purposeful, mission-minded Christians that their best work is something that they know nothing about. Edward also made this comment, which reverberates with insight for our own generation: "If we succeed without suffering it is because others suffered before us; if we suffer without succeeding, it is that others may succeed after us."

Antiprinciples

*B*ut is Adoniram's experience, hanging upside down in the muck, a seeming failure on every front, a way of thinking about leadership? I think it is part of the view. Judson went through some strange phases in his life, and he was not always a stable person. After the death of his wife and his daughter, and as he reflected on his experience as an upside-down prisoner, he went through a long period of self-doubt. He wondered if, even in his current trials, he had become a missionary through ambition, rather than humility. He destroyed all letters of commendation. He renounced the Doctor of Divinity given to him by Brown University. He gave all his savings and inheritance to the Baptist Board and asked that his salary be reduced by one quarter.

He survived the demeaning agonies of prison better than he did the death of his wife, Ann who had done everything for him while he was incarcerated. After her death, Judson retreated in isolation to a hut in the jungle and had a grave dug beside the hut. For days at a time, he sat beside the grave and thought about how he would look lying there. With his desire for cleanliness, the dirt of the grave must have been revolting to him, yet he thought about the fact that he would be there. He didn't feel as though he deserved the company of others. He went through a long, dark period before renewal came in his life. Do these times, which seem so feeble and unproductive, have a part to play as we talk about leaders?

I think these negative, seemingly unproductive factors do have a part to play in any discussion of leading, of accomplishing, and of influencing. We omit these factors at our own peril. If we talk about leadership, these negative factors, these "antifactors," must be discussed. If we state a principle, it is important to state the "antiprinciple." Recognizing the opposing principle or opposing truth sometimes helps us have a fuller understanding of the way before us. A different kind of power comes when we understand the principle and the opposing principle. For example, in particle physics, antimatter is a form of matter in which the property of each particle is the reverse of that in the usual matter of our universe. If a lump of matter were to meet a lump of antimatter, the two types of matter would release large amounts of energy. In the same way, if we extend the metaphor from physics, the leadership principles discussed in many books are like the matter of the universe — basic and important. The principles in this book are more like antimatter; in other words, they are the "antiprinciples" of leadership. We lose something when we forget the opposing principles. If we only speak about the evident principles of leadership, the matter of the universe, those strong principles eventually become dead matters, obvious and as cold as stone. But when you bring the principles of leadership together with the antiprinciples, large amounts of energy can be released. With these opposing principles in place, the kingdom becomes a little bit bigger.

This idea is not new. Martin Luther in the Reformation almost 500 years ago understood the idea of keeping two opposing principles together. We have almost lost Luther's way of understanding things, because his words against his opponents were so cutting. Granted that his harsh comments on all opponents — Catholics, Anabaptists, Muslims, and Jews — continue to be toxic for others. Still, he opened the Bible for others in an astonishing way, even for us today. Here is a famous example of his way of holding two opposing truths together. He began his writing on the freedom of the Christian by saying this: "A Christian is a perfectly free lord of all, subject to none. A Christian is a perfectly dutiful servant of all, subject to all." How can someone be both of these things?

In his own way, Luther kept reminding us that true things are a journey of keeping these opposing comments together. He felt the opposing truths or paradoxes came straight from the Word of God. Indeed, as Luther writes, we find that Christians are saints and at the same time sinners. This statement has become such a cliché, that we can't even hear what Luther is really saying. Luther also said that God is always revealed and God is always hidden. The Cross glorifies and the Cross humiliates. He consciously spoke in opposites: external and internal, before God and before people, flesh and spirit, law and gospel, promise and fulfillment. Matter and antimatter. Truth, so to speak, and an opposing truth. We can't really just synthesize the opposing principles. For Luther, heresy and wrong thinking came when you collapse those opposing truths. The attempts to collapse opposing truths were not just a temptation in his own time. Luther's approach, and the explosive reaction it received, irritated even those in his own period who were at first sympathetic. Erasmus, the great scholar of the time, is said to have once made this comment: "I am not going to be burned at the stake for one of Luther's paradoxes." In a way, these opposing truths become tools in the kit of the leader.

The Bible acknowledges this model of opposing truths. The Book of Proverbs tells you a number of things that you may do and then it will be well with you. The Book of Job explores what happens when you do the God-fearing activities and then things go terribly for you. I am glad that they are kept close together in the middle of the Bible and are separated only by the book composed totally of the lyrics of songs.

Jesus clearly understood how to place contradictory truths together. One must find life. One must lose life. In order to find your life you must lose it. When he talks about the Son of Man being lifted up in the Gospel of John, the reader only slowly realizes the double meaning of being honored and being lifted up on the Cross in terrible torture. The glorification becomes the peak of humiliation.

So we see that leaders share some strong principles for leadership. But it is important to hold to our heart the principles of another view, the antiprinciples. There are strong obvious heroes of leadership, and there are the quiet antiheroes, sometimes in the shadows. There are leaders and there are these others, these "unleaders," so to speak, those who exhibit some quality or embrace a path that is the opposite of what we expect in our leaders. There are some unleaders who seem to pull the leadership principles inside out. If we only think of the strong, bold, assertive principles, our views may get skewed or crooked, off-center. At worst, our views become slick and self-centered.

Then how are we supposed to lead? How do we move ahead in the times when we see our world falling apart, just as Adoniram Judson literally found his world flipped upside down? How do we put one foot in front of another in those times when the principles we thought we had learned don't work? As we proceed, what do we do when we find our feet where our head should be and our head where our feet should be?

Unlearning

*I*t's a big kingdom. In *Transitions; Making Sense of Life's Changes,* William Bridges believes that ancient stories can help us in our current lives. He paints an evocative picture of how the Greek hero Odysseus changes as a person, and consequently as a leader. In *The Odyssey,* Odysseus's three-week home journey becomes a ten-year home journey. He is not a young warrior. He is a middle-aged man with a nearly grown son, trying with great difficulty, to get home. Clearly, his return home is not going so well. Odysseus, the cunning and brilliant natural leader, with a history of successes in the past, now endures a process of attrition on his journey. He started with 12 ships; 6 were destroyed and then 3 more. Finally, he is down to one, manned by a few men. At the end, he is alone, his last boat sucked down by the whirlpool of Charybdis. "This king and hero, who began with a fleet of ships, leaves the scene like a child astride a log." At one point in the story, the proud Greek hero must do an unprecedented thing in order to live. Names are so important in the ancient world. He actually takes the name of "Nobody." The symbolism is heavy-handed to say the least.

Through this process, Odysseus finds another kind of courage, and Bridges calls Odysseus's journey a kind of "unlearning." Most leaders know that in their journey of life, they will sometimes have to unlearn the lessons of leadership that served them so well in the past. Strangely enough, Odysseus' expansion as a person came through this process of personal attrition, where the skills that previously served him so well came to nothing.

As we read the Bible, do we not often see a process of

unlearning in leaders? Abraham who is blessed must learn about famine. Jacob must become a runaway and use a rock as a pillow. Joseph must be a slave and then a prisoner in order to be a ruler. Moses must move from the palace to a desert in order eventually to lead. David must be treated as a criminal and even a homeless person with mental health issues, although he has already been anointed as king. For a while, each of these characters seems to be going on a journey of diminishment, rather than a journey of expansion. The stories are so familiar that we have forgotten them and what they are really saying to us. I think these are not just stories of what happened, but they are stories of what happens. In our time, we seem to view any kind of diminishment as evidence of a lack of any leadership ability whatsoever. The biblical characters tell a deeper kind of story. In the middle of their "unlearning," how would they have done at a leadership conference? Can you imagine Abraham in the famine or Moses in the wilderness leading a conference on goal achievement?

Think of Moses at a leadership conference after about 35 years in the desert. "Well, I started out pretty strong, had a good education and a lot of possibilities. But for a while now, I have just been a shepherd. Well, really for a pretty long time. Over three decades. No, I haven't really seen much professional advancement. What was your question? Should I go back to Egypt where there are more opportunities? Well, I am kind of in trouble with the law there. No, it was not a small thing. It was a pretty big crime. I don't want to go into the details. Yes, I guess you could say I am a felon there. No, I don't really see any future in that direction." What a loser! At that point in his life, his leadership break-out group would have hardly been a big attraction.

In some ways, Paul becomes the classic unleader. In 2 Corinthians, he looks as though he is against the ropes, challenged and belittled for his lack of presence and speaking ability (2 Corinthians 10: 10). For the time, it seems that his personality is just not very compelling. In response at one point, he almost proclaims himself unleader, in order to affirm his apostleship. He "brags" about escaping from a city in a basket (2 Corinthians 11:32–33). In our words, he was literally a "basketcase," hardly a propitious spin to put on your past. Why would he choose that particular incident and use it as a defense? Everyone in antiquity would know that the finest military award for valor was the *corona muralis* (Latin: "walled crown"). It was given to the one who was first up the wall in the face of the enemy. Paul's bragging moves in the opposite direction. He was the first one down. Then in response to his hyperspiritual opponents he tells about the time that God did *not* answer his prayer (12:8). He boasts in his weakness (12:9). He keeps saying the opposite of what you would expect: "for when I am weak, then I am strong" (12:10).

Even people from outside realized that Paul was living and espousing a life that seemed a bit upside down. Something had just gotten hold of him. When Paul was in Thessalonica, a group attacked the place where they lived. Listen to their language about Paul and Silas: "These men who have turned the world upside down have come here also" (Acts 17:6).

Jesus also preaches antiprinciples sometimes, principles from another view. In the Sermon on the Mount, before Jesus told the disciples to do anything, it seems as though He is helping them to see. We would expect to hear "blessed are the rich, blessed are those who laugh, blessed are the strong, blessed are the full." However, we hear, "blessed are the poor in spirit . . . blessed are those who mourn . . . blessed are the meek . . . blessed are those who hunger" (Matthew 5:3-6).

What a journey of unlearning for His disciples—blessing enemies, giving away to those who sue, looking happy during a fast, choosing the lowest seat. Of course, we know that this inversion in life is often true. We know in our heart that being a leader is not just a process of learning leadership principles. It is sometimes this process of unlearning. There is an old saying for leaders who are too confident that they know for certain the way to move ahead in life because of their past successes—"life has a board for every behind."

Paul understood that the entire life of Jesus was a kind of upside-down format for our own actions with others. When Paul spoke of Jesus, he instructed the Christians in a reversal of the normal surge toward influencing others. Instead of an upward path for Christ, Paul charted a sort of downward path to emptiness which might shock us if the words weren't so familiar—"Have this mind among yourselves which is yours in Christ Jesus, who, though he was in the form of God, did not count equality with God a thing to be grasped, but made himself nothing" (Philippians 2:5–7). This movement of unlearning flows from Jesus to His first disciples to the early Christians right to our growth today.

Slumping Toward the Kingdom

People who are true leaders know these alternative truths intuitively. Sometimes we normal people just need to be reminded. I remember in one of the darkest times of my work in church and community service in New York City, I went to hear a famous urban activist. My wife and I were working out of a storefront in an area flooded with homeless people and those living in abandoned buildings. I felt myself battered by needs and by people's destructive anger and by my own incompetence. I thought about my own "hardships." A man I had befriended tried to choke me on the street, grabbing my neck in anger with both hands on a hot afternoon. Another man to whom we gave food pulled a knife on me, and moved to cut up the people around me. A woman receiving clothing had tried to hit me with a board with a nail in it. The nail part missed me. Another man took a swing at me as I walked down the street. I felt exhausted and betrayed. I sat in the back of the auditorium and I could hardly speak. Like Paul, I was a true basket case.

I looked around the room and I saw that many of the urban workers looked as tired and battle scarred and weary as I felt. The person behind the podium talked about his success in ministry and how things continued to expand and about the things we ought to be doing in the city. He made us want to be on the cutting edge and to think big. He was a good speaker. His voice rose as he reached the climax of his talk. He told some stories of his success. Some of the people there were energized by the motivation given by the speaker. They had come to be pumped up by what could be, and they were. Yet as we left, I noticed that some of the listeners had slumped shoulders and looked the way I felt. I felt even more tired and discouraged, because I was not as good a thinker, or speaker, or leader as the person behind the podium. The man's very energy accentuated my own defeat. I just didn't feel as though I had the qualities the speaker was requiring. At that moment, I felt that I only had the opposite kind of qualities. The higher his voice rose, the lower I felt, as if I were in some kind of bipolar relationship with his preaching.

So there we were in the audience at the close of the meeting, the shadow people, the unleaders, slumping our way out of the auditorium, wallowing in the increased realization of our own inadequacies. The principles in this book are for those of us who sometimes feel that way. Again, I think that these antiprinciples are already known intuitively by great leaders. Those naturally great leaders won't need to read this book. The principles here are for the rest of us.

Even though most of us don't feel like leaders a lot of the time, we are all leaders in some form or other. If we describe leaders as people who influence others to achieve a goal, we are really in the realm of all of life. The mother is influencing her children. The eight-year-old is influencing her little brother who is six years old. The garbage collector is influencing his coworker as they collect garbage. The small group participant is influencing the other members, whether he or she is teaching or not. The 18-year-old drug dealer is teaching his 16-year-old cousin to do the same. The person who comes to church and looks for ways to be fed by the speaker, but does little else, is influencing others in the church without realizing it. From this perspective, we are all leaders and we might profit from thinking about how we are influencing others in this strange carnival of consciousness that swirls around us. In fact, none of the principles discussed in this book will necessarily provide techniques for a leader or an unleader to be more successful. The things discussed are really about becoming real human beings.

Most of us don't think of ourselves as leaders, and when we see how drastically we fail to live up to our ideas about leadership, or the ideas someone has given us about leadership, we get discouraged. Perhaps remembering the unleadership principles, which are so important in life, will help the rest of us who feel so "unleaderly" most of the time. From a faith context, such remembering and encouragement is very important. Discouragement is the work of that malevolent force in the universe, to take our courage, to accuse us, to *dis*courage us. The work of the Spirit of God, the unspeakable presence of His love, His Holy Spirit, is to give us courage, according to the Gospel of John, to *en*-courage us.

So if the leadership principles we sometimes hear seem too canned and, well, discouraging, perhaps it is time to follow some unleadership principles. Thinking in this way may protect us from entering a formulaic world. As we proceed, probably one of the most important questions we can ever ask is not "What are the principles?" As we shall see, that question should lead us to a better question, which is: "Is there anything, or anyone, behind the principles?"

Where Are You Going?

*W*e may find help in the Bible as we think about what learning means. Perhaps Peter was a natural leader. Perhaps Jesus saw something in him that was something special. The Bible doesn't spell that part out. But Peter was one who had some unlearning to do. Don't we all? A group of people I work with in Lower Manhattan did a study on "The Ten Stupid Things Peter Said." As we proceeded, we had to expand the number beyond ten. Peter was either lecturing Jesus at the wrong time, or making promises he wouldn't keep, or misunderstanding instructions and ending up cutting off somebody's ear. Even after the Resurrection, if you read Galatians, he was still having trouble getting things right.

But maybe in the end he got it. We don't hear how Peter died in the Bible, but the tradition about Peter's death may be revealing. Long after Jesus' own Crucifixion, Peter was in Rome, and it looked as though Peter would be arrested, so arrangements were made for him to run away. It seemed like the right thing to do. He had a precedent. As we saw, Paul had needed to make a quick exit from a city before too. All the Christian community advised him to do it. At the time, a departure seemed the inevitable leadership decision. As Peter fled the city, disguised and alone, he saw something startling. He saw Jesus himself entering the city. "Where are you going? (Latin: *Quo vadis?*)" Peter asked.

"To be crucified," Jesus answered.

"Are you going to be crucified again?" Peter asked.

"Yes, Peter, I am going to be crucified again."

Then Peter came to himself and returned to the city and knew returning was the thing to do at that time. No, there wasn't an easy answer and, no, Peter didn't procure some successful release because of turning back into the city. In fact, he was arrested as the others anticipated. As Peter was condemned, and they prepared to execute him by crucifixion, he looked at the cross as an old man. According to the story, he made one final, revealing request. He didn't feel worthy of being crucified right side up.

Even during his last hours on earth, Peter looked at the world from a different point of view. As a sign to the others, Peter asked to be crucified upside down.

principle #1
Stop Leading

A human life is like a single letter of the alphabet. It can be
meaningless. Or it can be part of a great meaning.

The writer Anne Lamott in *Traveling Mercies*
quoting an unnamed source from the Jewish
Theological Seminary

First Things First

As we saw in the introduction, Adoniram Judson was offered the best ministerial position in Boston, but his leadership career did not move in that direction. Instead he found himself hanging upside down by chains, with his head in the muck of a cruel prison.

Peter in the Gospels might have been a good fisherman, perhaps even a great fisherman, a world-class fisherman. Instead he followed a journey of unlearning with a teacher that changed his life, and the world has been instructed by reading the snippets concerning some of Peter's mistakes. In fact, his mistakes have probably encouraged us a lot more than his successes. In the end, to honor his leader, even Peter's execution was held upside down.

We might as well do first things first. Leaders can be seen as ones who influence others to achieve a goal. But the key question in leadership is not whether you are born a leader or not. The key question is not whether you can train to be a better leader. The key question is not whether you can locate the most important skills to be a leader, or whether you can secure the right mentor.

The key question is the painfully obvious one: Is there a God? If you don't think there is a God, the rest of the book won't make sense. Because if there isn't a God, of course we will need to train and make our own plans to get along as best we can in this world. If there is no God, techniques of leadership will be important as we package our abilities to achieve what we think is important. We can even forge our own values. To put it bluntly, we are on our own. Following one line of reasoning from this premise can lead to a view that if there is no God, it doesn't really matter what you do anyway. Others start with this premise that there may be no God and find great meaning within human experience. Whatever we decide, it is still the key question.

If there is a God, or even if we think there might be a God, it would be good if we could find out if God is the type of God that has any plans for us and others. The question of the type of God is really quite important. Our puny little goals won't matter much if there is something larger, or grander, or more complicated, or even smaller than we could imagine. Since the premise of this book is that there is a God, then learning to lead would have to start by learning to follow. We are starting in exactly the wrong place if we begin by talking about leading.

Regardless of how focused we are on our goals, we are constantly bombarded by the strangeness of life. For the unleader, that moment on Tuesday afternoon—when you open the window at work and hear a sparrow singing and stop to wonder at how odd the events of life really are—that moment may be the most important moment of the month. For no matter how much experience and wisdom we accumulate, life around us continues to be more unexpected than we expected. In Psalm 103:7, David uses a compelling phrase to talk about God and Moses, when he says that God "made known his ways to Moses, his acts to the people of Israel." The people saw the tangible acts God was doing, but God showed Moses His "ways." It is a humbling thing to ask God to show us His "ways." To say our thoughts are not His thoughts may be done in false humility, but at the very least the comment is an understatement. How would we possibly know God's ways?

An Unusual Inaugural Address

Abraham Lincoln is considered by many to be a great leader. He could speak eloquently for hours, and earlier in his life he often did. But his second inaugural address is only four paragraphs long. It is one of the most well known, and to me, one of the strangest speeches of all time. It was a time when our nation was viciously beaten down by war and needed the help of a strong leader. As Lincoln reflected on the horrors of the war that lay behind, and the challenges that lay ahead, he showed a humility that some leaders today lack. He said that each side in the war had thought the triumph would have been easier and had not anticipated the results:

> Both read the same Bible, and pray to the same God; and each invokes His aid against the other. It may seem strange that any men should dare to ask a just God's assistance in wringing their bread from the sweat of other men's faces; but let us judge not that we be not judged. The prayers of both could not be answered; that of neither has been answered fully. The Almighty has His own purposes.

What a remarkable speech for a leader to make at the closing of a war. What is most remarkable to me is the leader's public acknowledgment of so much, in the middle of a war, that he does not understand. The Almighty has His own purposes.

Cats Understanding Algebra

Once long ago I heard a cosmologist on television reflect on the keys to understanding the universe. He said something like this: "Perhaps we are simply not able to understand the operating principles of the universe. Perhaps it is like a cat trying to understand algebra."

That sentence has stuck with me for years. What if we are cats walking in a world of algebra? Proud assertions on our leadership skills would take on a different tenor then. Still, we have to do something. So what should we do?

In the discussion of plan or purpose, sometimes people will bring up the fact that humans are just hardwired to see a plan, whether there is one or not. It probably had survival value in the great flow of generations. A person will try to find a face in the moon, even though there isn't really one. But what if there were a God who was truly all-knowing and infinite? What if this God had an infinitely complex plan, perhaps a wonderful plan? Perhaps we would not be able in our limited perspective to truly understand it. Perhaps the face on the moon is more intricate than we can discern.

Anyone with a pet understands the limits of different levels of understanding. I have a wonderfully intelligent dog—at least *I* think he is wonderfully intelligent. But when I take him to the vet, my dog is not really going to understand why there is a person there in a strange-smelling coat who is sticking a needle into his little shivering body. I could never really explain to him about rabies and what the vaccination will do for him. It will be for his good, and could protect others, but it doesn't necessarily seem good at the time. He's just going to have to trust me on this one, and let me hold his head, and, in a sense, just obey me.

The world is certainly more complex than some people with a plan realize, and it is often hard to evaluate what is really the best for us and for others. Nassim Nicholas Taleb, a theorist on probability, indicates that humans often are not even equipped to evaluate what leadership is. Here is a thought-experiment he proposes:

> "Assume that a legislator with courage, influence, intellect, vision, and perseverance manages to enact a law that goes into universal effect and employment on September 10, 2001; it imposes the continuously locked bulletproof doors in every cockpit (at high costs to the struggling airlines) — just in case terrorists decide to use planes to attack the World Trade Center in New York City. . . . The legislation is not a popular measure among the airline personnel, as it complicates their lives. But it would certainly have prevented 9/11. The person who imposed locks on cockpit doors gets no statues in public squares, not so much as a quick mention of his contribution in his obituary."

Taleb implies that we are often not even able to recognize leadership that avoids terrible things. We more easily recognize leaders who clean up messes, although the one who could completely avoid the disaster would be a far more valuable leader. Taleb concludes, "We humans are not just a superficial race . . . we are a very unfair one."

He also writes extensively about leaders who have gained great wealth or fame through the workings of chance. These leaders were just as hardworking and intelligent and virtuous as many others but got their recognition due to chance. Yet once they have gained the good fortune, they look back and tell others, or write books, about what they did that made them so successful. Analysts may attribute their achievement to childhood experiences. The biographer might dwell on the wonderful role models the parents were. Others stress their strong work ethic. Yet in actuality, none of these factors were the cause of the person's success. Some of Taleb's work is quite convincing, and his writings help us consider some of our leaders in quite a different light.

In some ways, we may not have a clue what leadership is. Maybe we never will. Perhaps every person, regardless of even high degrees of competence in leadership, has had the feeling that the world is too vast and inexplicable and terrible and wonderful for them. So if there is a God, then learning to lead might mean learning to listen.

The World Will Think Them Useless

A French spiritual director in the eighteenth century, Jean-Pierre de Caussade understood the vastness of God's purpose. He instructed the visitation sisters under his care in the obedience of the present moment. He talked about those who surrendered totally to God: "For them there are no plans, no longer any clearly marked paths." These people, he says, will sometimes be discarded in a corner and neglected by others. They are trusting that they will serve God in His own way. "Often they will not know for what purpose," he said, "but God knows it well. The world will think them useless." Letting go of the reins of leading our lives will seem incomprehensible to those who think that what we see now is all there is. But as those truly surrendered to God continue in this way, "these souls pour out infinite blessings on people who may never have heard of them, of whose existence they are themselves unaware." A strong formulaic understanding of what God wants will miss this movement in the real complexity and richness of life.

Jean-Pierre de Caussade even prays a different kind of prayer. It is a prayer that recognizes that our confident plans may be way off course. He prays this way to Divine Love: "Mystify us, arouse and confuse us. Shatter all our illusions and plans so that we lose our way, and see neither path nor light until we have found you." He shows this different way to approach life, where sometimes our "unlearning" is as important as our learning.

Some people delude themselves, I think, and believe that if they just had the right information and enough information, they would be able to make the right decisions for themselves and for others. We are racing into a new world of thought, and it is hard for us to even think about how exponentially things are changing right now. Every few years, our capacity to retrieve information doubles through technological advance, and yet our ability to make meaningful decisions has not kept pace. Paradoxically, we often seem and feel more confused. We find ourselves sucked into this meaningless flow of trivial and banal information. We may feel as though we have less and less capacity to sort out what is important in order to make decisions for ourselves, our family, our church, our city, our nation, our world. Instead of our minds getting sharper and clearer, we feel overwhelmed and inundated by this seemingly endless capacity to retrieve information. How should we proceed?

Get the First Button Right

*I*n our ministry in the Lower East Side, we have a saying. Get the first button right. In other words, when you button your shirt, you must get the top button aligned properly. Otherwise all the other buttons, as you go down the line to button them, will be all messed up. When we talk about following rather than leading, in some ways this is the question we have to answer. Am I going to have that first button focus on God, or focus on my own plan that I will implement? Jesus talked about it—without referring to buttons. He simply said, "But seek first the kingdom of God and his righteousness, and all these things will be added to you." In my mind, I visualize that first button, the kingdom of God, and then all the rest of the buttons just naturally line up.

As a pastor, I often feel that people bring me their messed up shirt of a life. All the buttons are off center down close to their belly button, and they want me to counsel them so that they can fix that. I can be a listener concerning the messed-up buttons around their naval. But what I see is that they didn't get the first button right. This is the language I hear when people choose some other button to do first: "Well it's gotten really complicated. I'm in a gray area and I don't know what to do. I don't know why life is so confusing. How can I believe in a God who allows these things to happen?" You get the picture. Sometimes the person is even angry at God. The Bible in Proverbs 19:3 puts it this way: "When a man's folly brings his way to ruin, his heart rages against the LORD." We are so quick to set up our own plan, and then get secretly mad at the universe when it doesn't work.

How Is Your Way Working?

For 25 years I have worked with people who are transient and often sleep in the park, or wherever they can find a place. I remember meeting one old friend in the park recently. He looked terrible. He had lost his job. He had gone to jail. He had alienated the last shreds of his family. He owed people money. He had been drinking. Perhaps he felt like Frank Sinatra. After explaining all of these things, he puffed up his chest and said with some pride, "Well, you know me, pastor. I had to do it *my* way."

I quietly told him, "I don't think your way is really working so great." I think I hurt his feelings. All of us reach those moments of insight in our lives. If you are leading out of your own plan, how is your way working? If it isn't working so great, maybe it is time to go back to the first button, and consider if there are other options.

The Manual for Unleaders

For me, Genesis is a book that gives us instruction on leadership and unleadership. It is kind of a manual for unleaders. We leave the world of Taleb's theories of randomness, but in terms of how much people really understand, the world of Genesis is very similar. To think of an ancient and familiar example in the Genesis story, take Noah. Noah has gotten bad press in some circles, or has been relegated to a children's story with a little toy boat and pairs of little animals. Or he is the subject of comedic monologues or movies, where the main character is totally surprised that God speaks.

Yet the biblical Noah, within the framework of his own story, is a much subtler character. The Bible says he walked with God (Genesis 6:9). This is the key. In my mind, I suppose that this long process of living with God was the reason that God chose Noah. Noah listened, and in small instructions he obeyed. His mind was open to guidance in the small things. He had learned a habit of following. So, when God told him to do this absurd, ridiculous, astonishing thing, to build a boat in a dry area, Noah had a history of a relationship. He knew the voice of God, and he could obey. He could take the ridicule of others for a long, long time.

In terms of results, in the context of the story, what leader has had a more critical impact? What leader had to stand up to such pervasive ridicule? And for so long? Obviously, there were other, more persuasive leaders at the time, leaders who had larger followings than Noah did. The number of people who followed Noah was extremely small, just his own family, but those people were critical for the survival of so many. Yet Noah could not have understood all the implications in terms of seeing the long view. Noah was probably a cat trying to understand algebra. At the very least, the story should make us pause to blink.

After the story of Noah, it seems as though the people make a bold leadership decision in order to avoid being "scattered abroad." They decide to build a city and a tower. It sounds like a good idea. It was a disaster, and accomplished the very thing they were trying to avoid—being scattered. So much for bold leadership (Genesis 11:1-9).

Abraham in Genesis is the next story. What possible way could Abraham understand what would happen when God told him to go to the place that He would show him? God's purpose for Abraham spanned generations, and from the Christian perspective, the purpose spanned thousands of years to a purpose that we as readers today cannot yet fully see. In each generation, we continue to be amazed at the promise that "in you all the families of the earth shall be blessed" (Genesis 12:3).

The reader of Genesis has an expanding view, depending on what context the story is placed in. Abraham's obedience in following is a connection that spreads beyond his own life. We move from Abraham to Isaac and to Jacob, and eventually to the story of Joseph. The reader is totally involved with Joseph's journey in Genesis from prison to power, so that he can be the answer to the hunger problems of so many. But as we read carefully, we become aware of the words of the brothers.

It is Joseph's brother Judah who says to the father that they must return to Egypt for food—"we will arise and go, that we may live and not die, both we and you and also our little ones" (Genesis 43:8). Slowly the reader remembers that Judah is the forefather of King David. His children, "our little ones," must not starve to death, or there would be no King David. As the centuries pass, the Christian reader realizes that Jesus is the descendent of David. I am writing these sentences more than 3,000 years removed from the story of Joseph because of the influence of Jesus. If Judah and his children had died (and they would have if Joseph hadn't gone to prison, according to the story)—well, it would have been a "Back to the Future" moment on the grandest of scales. Everything afterward could have been erased. How could Abraham have understood all of that process? The flow of time continues through him and beyond us, and we yet do not see how things will be shaped. Could he have ever guessed that the faiths of the population of half the world look back to him as a foundational figure? We still don't know all that is coming from Abraham's act of following, though we gather in churches and synagogues and mosques and talk about it.

This idea of being a follower of God was very important even to Jesus in the Book of John. In a way, Jesus didn't talk about His leadership plans. I have noted in my Bible that 47 times, Jesus said He never did anything or said anything without the Father. Jesus had developed the habit of following. In the end, He said that as the Father had sent Him, so He sends us. If a leader is someone who truly influences people, it slowly dawns on us, that to follow might be the way to really lead.

Sometimes I play the "what if" game. In the Book of Acts, Ananias in Damascus received a vision telling him to go to a particular address in Damascus (a street called Straight) and help a certain Saul of Tarsus. What if Ananias had responded differently? He could have said, "I am not sure that was a vision, and I have many important things to do today. I don't have time to go to the other side of town on a wild goose chase after Saul. I know that villain and what he has done to Christians, and it would be gravely imprudent to visit him."

What would have happened to Saul, later named Paul, if Ananias had refused to go and pray for him? Would there have been no Paul, no missionary outreach from him to Rome and beyond? Would half of the New Testament, the part about him or written by him, have to go? I am sure Ananias could not have imagined all that came about from his small visit on a busy day. He couldn't have seen the whole plan, yet he put aside his plan and obeyed (Acts 9:10-18).

Twigs on a River

True leadership must be critically suspicious of its own goals. Once we begin to listen to God, even the idea of leadership starts to undermine itself. When we read the disturbing stories in the Bible, sometimes our ideas on leadership seem to implode.

Jonah in the Old Testament is an example of someone who certainly had his own ideas. He was committed not to go to the Assyrians. Because of the savage cruelty of Assyrian rule during this period, some Bible students have said that, to the Jewish people, they were emotionally like the "Nazis" of the ancient world. But his plan didn't lead to the leadership that God had in mind. And even when he partially followed and went to the city of the people he hated, he still didn't get it right. We end the story with Jonah's little suicidal monologue, but we get a glimpse of what God wants for those city dwellers, and what God wants for us. Incidentally, we even learn what God thinks of the cattle. Just take a moment and read the last phrase of the book. Once again, as we read the Bible carefully, we see that God's plan is more vast and intricate than we had imagined. Even a casual reader of the Bible realizes that if the Bible is truth, it is not in any way exhaustive truth. It doesn't tell us everything about everything. We don't even get to see how Jonah responds to God. And why are those cattle so important?

Jonah had a little unlearning he had to do. Jonah's goal of avoiding Nineveh hadn't worked out so well. He had to go through the fish and even afterward, he insisted on pouting and moaning to God. God clearly had plans of His own. Jonah's journey must have seemed so upside down to him. Oddly enough, Jonah didn't ascend into some high heaven to begin to understand what God was doing; he descended to the lower parts of the ocean, far below sea level. It was there in the depths of the ocean, in his greatest isolation and need that he got a bit of understanding. Even so, at the end of the story, we get a hint that maybe, just maybe, Jonah had the chance to see things right side up. But Jonah would have to stop leading out in his own little plans. We are not told the ending of his story.

We talk as if we are the captains of our ships, the masters of our fate, but the complexity of our real experience in life calls into suspicion such an approach. We think we have so much freedom to set the course of our own goals but, in reality, we are just twigs on a mighty rushing river, pretending to be captains.

principle #2
Forget Results

All service ranks the same with God.

Robert Browning

Master Language and Servant Language

*O*nce upside-down leaders have stopped leading, they might as well forget results too. Just think of it, if we really are the cat trying to understand algebra, then our methods of evaluating results are probably pretty flimsy. Duh.

Among other reasons, people read Oswald Chambers's devotional book *My Utmost for His Highest* because it challenges our presupposition that we necessarily have any clue about what God's purpose is. In talking about the disciples, he makes this comment:

> We are apt to imagine that if Jesus Christ constrains us, and we obey Him, He will lead us to great success. We must never put our dreams of success as God's purpose for us; His purpose may be exactly the opposite. We have an idea that God is leading us to a particular end, a desired goal; He is not. The question of getting to a particular end is a mere incident. What we call the process, God calls the end.

We walk on flimsy ground when we pretend to know what God's complete goal is in a particular situation. We might have even seen the wrong thing as the goal.

The thought that getting to a mere goal was incidental to God came to me late in life. Our ministry was building a new building in Manhattan. To stretch our money we were using a lot of volunteer teams and the owner was the contractor. This meant lots of complicated construction decisions for me and the other staff who often felt totally unprepared for what was required.

I remember one summer when the basement of the half-built building was flooded and neighbors were angry about the potential for mosquitoes. Another man, who lived in a neighboring squat, was angry at the possible noise of our air conditioners and came drunk and cursing, throwing things at a group of volunteers who had come from outside the city to help. On the other side of the construction site, at the same time, a man was taking us to court because he saw a delivery person double park in front of our fire hydrant. In the same period, several of the construction providers were woefully delayed, and we were having trouble getting them back on the job. To top things off, our financial resources were running just a bit on the slim side.

I began to fantasize about receiving a check for two million dollars in the mail. Why couldn't we build a building as fast as Donald Trump? I felt out of my element and worn out, so I took a subway to a place on the outskirts of the city where I could just be alone and walk. As I walked, the logic of my situation hit me. God could build a building just like that. He could turn things on a dime whenever He wanted to do so. The circumstances, and the goal of building a building, were all that I could see, and I was discouraged. But that goal was not really as important to God.

I thought about how sometimes in the ancient world the word for "name" could almost be translated "character," because the name shows the essence of the person. I thought about how God told Abraham that he would make his name (character) great so that he would be a blessing (Genesis 12:2). Then it hit me. God was working on my character and the character of our church and the character of the other people who were working on the project. Through this project that seemed agonizingly slow to me, He was teaching us dependence on Him when resources were low, endurance when things went more slowly than we thought, and humility as others mocked us for our seeming inability to finish in a timely manner. It struck me like a rocket—God was teaching us to not hesitate in faith when obstacles came on. That was at least part of His goal in this project. My preoccupation with timelines and goals and a tangible building were almost beside the point to God. Now, years later, the building is complete and paid for. The missed timelines and misunderstandings are almost all forgotten. But what God did in the character of our church, and in my friends, and in me, remains.

Jesus warned His students about looking for the outward results. He said, "The kingdom of God is not coming with signs to be observed, nor will they say, 'Look, here it is!' or 'There!' for behold, the kingdom of God is in the midst of you" (Luke 17:20–21). According to Jesus, looking for outward, visible signs could be a distraction. It is something else happening, right in His students' midst, or even within them, that He calls the kingdom of God. Looking too far outside ourselves would mean missing the real action.

A wise old urban pastor used to encourage my wife and me in those early days of our ministry in New York City. When we looked at the failures in our work, at the wasteland of our labors with few results and little productive goals, he would nod his head and respond.

> "Remember, results and goals and objectives are the words of master language. But you were not called to be masters. Obedience and faithfulness and responsiveness are servant language. That is your calling. It is for your Master to think about productivity. Your job is to be faithful and obedient."

When Should We Really Evaluate?

*I*t is hard to evaluate success, and it is even harder to know when to evaluate it. How could Noah evaluate success, and when? After 10 years, 20 years, after 100 years? After a thousand years? It is the same with Abraham. I continue to wonder if he ever dreamed how important he was in God's scheme of things. Even today, we are still learning how important he was. I suppose I wouldn't be sitting here at this laptop in this place, surrounded by these Christian books, without Abraham. How could he have dreamed of what has happened through him?

We are informed of our inability to make judgments in this area in Ecclesiastes. God has planted eternity in the human heart. But even so, humans are not able to see the whole scope of what God is doing from beginning to end (see Ecclesiastes 3:11). We may be able to see a small part of what God is doing, but the Bible says that we are not *able* to see the whole scope of what God is doing.

Like the fish that doesn't see the water around it, leaders fail to remember our inability sometimes because it is so obvious. The truth of the matter is, that despite our best intentions as leaders, our idea of success can be very shortsighted. We are simply not capable of seeing things from the beginning to the end.

A long time ago, my wife and I spent two years teaching in the Baptist college in Hong Kong. We had many ear-opening conversations with students and friends there. At that time and afterward, I became aware of this very common story. It is the story of the Chinese farmer. Once upon a time a farmer's horse ran away. All his neighbors came around and said, "Oh, that is too bad." The farmer shrugged his shoulders and said, "How do you know?" Because the next day, the horse returned, and it brought with it an entire herd of wild horses. All the neighbors gathered around, and said, "Oh, that is wonderful." The farmer shrugged his shoulders and said, "How do you know?" Because the next day the farmer's oldest son was breaking one of the horses and he was thrown and badly broke his leg. The neighbors came around and said, "Oh, that is too bad." Once again the farmer shrugged his shoulders and said, "How do you know?" Because the next day the king's representative came to draft all the young men in the village to an unpopular war in the north . . . and the story continues.

For me, the point of the story is that in reality we will never really know what is good or bad, successful or unsuccessful, until the last ticking of the clock when time and space end. We really don't see the whole scope. Cause and effect may have unforeseen accumulating effects, and very often unintended consequences. If we too boldly chart what we think the goals should be and make evaluations on the results of immediate actions, we may just be pretending to be captains.

Thomas Cahill has written some thoughtful books about different parts of our civilization. In his book *The Gifts of the Jews,* he makes an insightful comment. He indicates that one of the greatest things that the Jews brought to our understanding was that God could work through a series of generations. The careful linear attention to genealogies that has bored generations of Bible readers is an indication of this sense that God is working His plan through time. Such a view is in contrast to the more circular views of surrounding ancient cultures, where everything is happening again and again in a seasonal rhythm. As we think about the complexity of family systems and the journey of tracking causes and the puzzle of those unintended consequences, this comment seems on the mark. Even if we look at the track of our entire life, we may not really see what God is doing.

Abraham and Sarah to Isaac and Rebecca to Jacob and Leah to David and Bathsheba to Jesus to us. Who would have thought it? This direction is part of the "meta-narrative" of Christians all over the world. We are told that the number of Christians is increasing in the world at large. They now comprise perhaps up to a third of the population of the world. Confident leaders should take a moment and think on this movement, and like the kings of old in Isaiah, they should shut their mouths in amazement because of it.

Time is important, so when will we judge the effectiveness of a leader? For example, in his own time, Caesar Augustus must have been rated as the most important person and the greatest leader of the known world. How things change. Now we date his life by the birth of a child from a peasant family in one of the most insignificant outposts of his realm. You would have never guessed it during that peasant's lifetime, nor in most of the world for a long time afterwards, but now we see Augustus eclipsed by the influence of that man.

We See Dimly in the Present . . .

During difficult times in the civil rights movement, Martin Luther King Jr. would refer to this puzzle concerning history and time. Sometimes he would quote this poem, *The Present Crisis* by James Russell Lowell:

> Truth forever on the scaffold,
> Wrong for ever on the throne —
> Yet that scaffold sways the future, and, behind the dim unknown,
> Standeth God within the shadow, keeping watch above his own.

King would remind himself and others that in looking at immediate results, truth may look as though it is dying, and wrong looks as if it is enthroned forever. The poem reminds us that God, out of sight, within the shadow, may have other plans. But Lowell continues in the poem, and really puts his finger on the sense of what is happening around us. He writes, "We see dimly in the Present what is small and what is great, Slow of faith how weak an arm may turn this iron helm of fate." The unleader becomes more and more aware that we see very imperfectly in the present time what is really small and what is really great.

Perhaps this insight is one of the reasons that J. R. R. Tolkien's books and also the movies touch such a deep chord in people. In *The Lord of the Rings*, the one ring, which brings such tremendous power when used, holds the promise of such wonderful results. Using it tempts the corrupt nature in all of us. The good person will want to use it for good at first, but in the end, the power taints the person's being toward ever-increasing evil. In the story, all the fate of the great kings and warriors and wise ones hangs on the fate of one small hobbit, a Halfling, who must carry the ring to the heart of the evil land. One would assume all eyes would be on the massive battles waged by great heroes with great weapons, but in reality these battles are decoys. Everything depends on the actions of one everyday little hobbit, journeying on unnoticed ways.

Tolkien thought a lot about the strange nature of our world. In the middle of some of the worst of World War II, he wrote this to his son:

> "the future is impenetrable especially to the wise, for what is really important is always hid from contemporaries, and the seeds of what is to be are quietly germinating in the dark in some forgotten corner, while everyone is looking at Stalin or Hitler." In one sense, these are hard words, for the wise are sometimes the ones who think they understand. But there is a source of encouragement in these words forr the unleader, because when things may seem darkest, God may be standing within the shadows working in some forgotten corner to turn things around.

Unspoken on the surface, we sometimes feel that the bold decisive decision is the one that gets results. At times this insight is true. Yet it is fascinating to read about the process that George Muller used as he helped in providing for thousands of orphans at a time. He never asked anyone for help, only prayed to God. He would sense God leading him to step out in a certain area, but he would slowly, quietly, pray and explore how God would provide for what was needed. He never lost patience, and from the outside he may have looked too deliberate, but he wanted to make sure he was being obedient to God, not to some idea he had about what a leader should do.

I recently read again parts of George Muller's meticulous faith journal as he prays about building a new building specifically for orphans during the middle of the nineteenth century. He tells only the smallest group of people about his desire, and prays only to God about it, writing what he learns. At one point, he praises God because he has waited 447 days for the amount needed to start the building. He is so thankful for the blessing he has received by trusting God and waiting patiently. Having been involved in a building project myself, I am stunned by Muller's restraint when the needed results seem so eminently urgent.

As unleaders mature, they often understand that some decisions need time. To the obedient unleader, decisions are to be soaked in God's Word, encouraged and confirmed by those you respect in the community of faith, sensitive to the moving of God's circumstances, waiting and attentive to the voice we hear behind us saying that this is the way. As the person walks along this way, the results that seemed so important at the beginning may fade, and some other directions may emerge. Results can be deceiving to any leader. Quick results don't necessarily mean the leader has been effective. No result doesn't necessarily mean the leader has been ineffective.

In fact, humans may have a very difficult time evaluating real results. We are swayed by seeing things happen in our own time, but relatively unable to evaluate some things that happen over a long period of time. How do we evaluate the effectiveness of a church? For example, a particular gifted personality draws a large number of people to a church and they build a huge auditorium for all the people. The compelling personality moves on and the church dwindles and eventually the auditorium is sold to a dance hall. Next to the large church is a small church that has been present and active for a hundred years before the gifted personality preached next door, and it is active for a hundred years after the large church dies. Which church affected more people and which church was more productive? While the gifted personality is present, it is very hard for humans to evaluate the results of the small church. We aren't really equipped to see things in that way.

Results as a Trap

Seeing the world in terms of results can become a trap, a grid through which everything is viewed. One single indicator of success becomes the standard for everything, whether that indicator is grades or money or career promotion or sports achievement or something else. I read recently an old story from years ago, where a man killed himself because he had 50 million dollars and in an economic downturn he lost 40 million dollars. The person reporting the story asked in a quite logical way this question—why would a man kill himself who had 10 million dollars? That amount of money would sound pretty good to most of us. Here, however, is an example of how focusing on a particular result can make a person lose all perspective.

Perhaps I sound morbid, but I think sometimes a preacher should remind people that we are all going to die. We are all of us, in the end, going to lose everything. We will lose health, property, and every relationship on this earth that we value. We may lose it all suddenly, or gradually, but we are all going to lose it all. Unless the world experiences the end of time and space as we know it by God's act, this loss of everything is not optional. The fact should remind us to hold a light grasp on all the outward, visible results in life. The Hebrew prophets had a word for trying to hold on too tightly to some relationship or visible, tangible product or result in our lives. They called it *idolatry*. Idolatry is a word that sounds so religious, but the truth of the matter is that no person or thing or indicator can really bear the weight of being our ultimate desire or concern. They will all, even the good things, be in the end unable to bear that weight. Putting all our emphasis on some form of tangible results, even spiritual results, can turn into a form of idolatry, and skew our perspective on life.

Here is another danger of being a result-driven leader. We forget people and we become salespeople. Even people become a means to a result. Paul talks about this in Second Corinthians. He says, "For we are not, like so many, peddlers of God's words, but as men of sincerity, as commissioned by God, in the sight of God we speak in Christ" (2 Corinthians 2:17). Focusing with intensity on results can make you a "peddler," instead of the leader you wanted to be.

We've all noticed this phenomenon at some time or other. I've noticed it in myself. When we focus only on some result, even a person can become an object, someone we need to sell something to. When we have said the exact same thing many times, our voice can take on a slickness, an inauthenticity. Everybody notices it. You hear it in the tone of telemarketers on the phone sometimes. You hear it in the voice of a salesman who is making a pitch for us to buy some product. You hear it in the voice of an evangelist or pastor who has spoken the same words the same way too often. Perhaps they are only thinking of the results, even very good results. Perhaps they have forgotten the real person with a very unique set of feelings and emotions and personality. Without taking care, the preacher can become a peddler, just like the others.

Let me give you an example from what I am doing right now. In writing, I want to get across the danger of making results our aim, but personally I have also made a commitment to myself to finish so many words today before I go to a movie tonight. My counter on my computer says I have 353 more words to go to get to my goal, and the clock is ticking. If I keep thinking this way I will forget you, the reader, and the truth I am trying to communicate. I begin to think about reaching a certain subjective number of words. In reality the number is completely arbitrary. Even this paragraph will help me achieve that numerical goal. But it doesn't make you feel so great, does it? Don't tell me you've never been caught up in this kind of numerical goal-oriented thinking. It's really crazy when you stop to think about it — it's a trap.

I see this result-driven process happening all the time in the city, especially in social services. I see a number of systems that started out with the best of intentions and, in spite of themselves, become dehumanizing. It's a classic story. A social worker becomes a social worker because he or she sincerely wants to help people. This idealistic person, along with other idealistic people, are fit into a system that gives them a caseload that is far beyond their capacity—a system that pressures them to complete all that goes with that load. Affirmation comes from the system in getting a certain number of reports in at the right time. Clients are disappointing and don't fulfill expectations as the daily pressure mounts. Fatigue, burnout, and finally cynicism sets in. After a few years, the young social worker has become a different person, hardened to the realities before that individual by the very nature of the social work structure. Some social workers are able to transcend this trap, but it is hard to see how they do it.

People tell me about social workers who have become monsters because the client's life didn't fit the system and what was needed. The social worker didn't intend to start that way, but the required forms of the system drove the worker to it. It can happen with a preacher, a missionary, a teacher, a business person, a scientist, a medical person, or anyone. The results have taken over the person's life and the focus on results has changed them. They didn't even know it was happening.

At Graffiti Community Ministry, we have sometimes joked about how long it will take a new worker to get calloused. I don't suppose that what we did was right. At times in the past, we have taken guesses on how long it will take the wide-eyed, loving person, the one who has volunteered to help with providing emergency clothes for people, to snap. Sure, Jesus says to us in the end that when He was naked, you clothed Him, so the work of providing clothes at some level is deep and powerful. But we watched to see how long it would take for the new worker to break. It sometimes took only a few months for the originally sweet-talking worker to be shouting in fury, "I gave you a stocking cap last week and you know the rules! Now stop pounding on the door!"

Leaders in ministry can also be engulfed in the power of their own successful results. Sometimes they forget who they are and become an office monkey instead of a minister, or a quisling to the call of speaking, instead of a preacher. Some leaders sound as though the delivery system for sharing the Great News is far more important than the news itself. If we only worked harder, the delivery system would finally be perfected and the results would be better. But when the transforming Great News is working, it will draw people like the smell of steak cooking in the backyard of a hungry neighborhood. It is the product, so to speak, not the delivery system, that was meant to bring results.

Learning Not to Overshoot the Mark

Sometimes people who aim so vigorously for successful results overshoot the mark. We catch a glimpse of how these things can work even in our own American history. Doris Kearns Goodwin's book on Abraham Lincoln, *A Team of Rivals*, gives us a good window into what can happen, even on the political stage. As Lincoln was running for the Senate, at one point he was a few votes short of winning the election. The other nonslavery candidate, who had drawn only a small number of votes, merely needed to throw his votes in Lincoln's favor. Then a non-slavery candidate would have won. Yet the other nonslavery candidate refused to do so. Hence a long stream of votes and negotiation ensued. In the end, Lincoln said he would throw all his votes to the other candidate, who just had a handful, because it was more important having someone with non-slavery principles elected. Lincoln's representatives were so upset they refused to take the message to the other candidate.

In terms of immediate personal results, Lincoln looked as though he had made a very poor choice and had added another failure to a long list of failed attempts. Yet if we follow the flow of history, here is another part of the story. The campaign manager of the other candidate was extremely impressed with what Lincoln had done, and he never forgot it.

Later that campaign manager was on the Republican National Committee to choose where the Republican Convention would be for the 1860 convention. He calmly suggested, "What about Chicago? That would be a nice neutral place." Lincoln was hardly on the radar as a potential candidate. The manager convinced the others that Chicago was the ideal place, and then he got cheap railroad tickets for trips all over Illinois. Lincoln's supporters streamed in and helped change the course of history. One wonders what would have happened, if Lincoln had focused on his own personal results in the earlier election.

Adoniram Judson wanted results for his preaching in Burma. For a number of years he had no converts, and even at the end of his life, there were only a relatively small number of churches in Burma. Now Myanmar (Burma) has the third largest number of Baptists in the world, behind the United States and India.

Perhaps you are in a small, insignificant place, where you have seen few results. Hey, we just don't know yet. Give yourself a couple of years. Or maybe a couple of centuries. Or maybe a handful of millennia.

principle #3
Make No Plans

I am done with great things and big plans, great institutions and big success. I am for those tiny, invisible, loving, human forces that work from individual to individual, creeping through the crannies of the world like so many rootlets, or like the capillary oozing of water, which, if given time, will rend the hardest monuments of pride.

—American psychologist and philosopher
William James

It May Be a Jazz Concert

As we go through life, some people make their plans as though they are scoring a symphony. This approach can work very well in some circumstances. Sometimes in life, on the other hand, it is better to approach things as if it were a jazz concert, improvising on the way, listening to what is happening as the music develops.

However, in thinking in terms of leadership, we often make the wrong plans. To say "make no plans," does not mean avoiding decisions. Whatever we do in life, even refusing to make any decisions, is a decision. The pitches keep coming in life, and sometimes we are required to take a swing. Refusing to swing is simply another decision. But for the unleader, making no plans has another meaning. It simply means intentionally deciding to start with God rather than starting with our own intentions, goals, and schemes.

One radio preacher put it well as he talked about his own time of prayer with God. "Here am I, a little guy who knows practically nothing, in the presence of the Someone who knows everything. Why am I doing all the talking?"

Our minds are filled with the plans we think we should enact for other people. It is astonishing the things we do sometimes, rushing into people's lives, meaning no harm, holding on to our plan. A while ago, an older woman was close to my wife, Susan, and myself. It was clear to me that she had been deeply hurt, abused, or brutalized somehow as a child. Because of my seminary and psychology training, I felt she needed to talk about those deep problems with someone. At one point she asked me to counsel her. I had a plan, and I tried in many ways to help her uncover these terrible traumas I had diagnosed in her. But in reality, she never did reveal those kinds of things to me or to my wife. She passed away many years ago. I still do not know if some horrible event or series of events actually shaped her childhood. That kind of diagnosis came from the training of my generation and my background.

As I think back about our times together, I think now what she was really asking from my wife and myself was simple friendship, not some psychotherapist's relationship. We received that gift from each other in spite of my plans for her as a pastor, with all my reforming ways. She was a draining person in some ways, but Susan and I were surprised at how much we missed her after she died. I think one of the things that will strike future ages about our own time is the abundance of psychological terms we use with their own special diagnoses of life's problems. These diagnoses almost always suggest a certain kind of plan to fix things. This psychological language comes out even in our sermons. I wonder what future generations will think of us and our psychoanalyzing plans for others.

Positioning

The Bible brings a certain worldview with it. In it God says He will teach us and instruct us in the way that we should go. The Bible is also full of people making all kinds of wrong plans. Abraham had a strong plan for Ishmael. He was wrong. David had quite a plan to build a temple. He had to be stopped because he had blood on his hands. The ways God speaks are many and varied. David's most important quality was not his ability to make grand plans, but the willingness to adjust to what God said. Peter had a plan for what kind of Messiah Jesus would be, one lacking the suffering and crucifixion. Jesus had to rebuke that part of Peter's intention. Peter had to make adjustments. Peter had a lot of other plans that kept getting blunted.

Adjusting to what God says is a quality of the heart. As a boy, one of my sons got fearlessly involved with playing chess as we lived in Manhattan. He could beat me without even paying attention. I learned a new word—*positioning*. In good chess, the key to winning is positioning the pieces in a strong way. If a pawn is positioned in the proper place, it can significantly control an area and consequently the game. By positioning the pieces properly, a player has a strong posture in the game and will eventually win.

I like to think of God as positioning us. Of course we would not really be able to understand the complexity of the way He positioned us. Our real-life positions would be in a game that would make three-dimensional chess look like kindergarten. But whether we are a pawn, a queen, or a king, the key issue for us is to be in the position we are assigned. I can imagine a master chess player positioning the pieces in a way that a beginning player would not even understand. And how could you possibly understand if you were actually in the pawn's position, crowded by larger pieces, unable to see the whole board?

Leadership requires the humility of realizing one might be a pawn set in a position where one doesn't even begin to understand the confluent resources. If we were to give the pawn a thinking life, we might even say it needs to be "enduring" in the place it has been placed. That sounds almost like the New Testament.

Oswald Chambers would have understood the idea of positioning. We know him as the writer of the remarkably successful book, *My Utmost for His Highest*. As a young man he was artistic and intense in his heart for God. He was a student at the prestigious University of Edinborough, but he felt led to leave it to join a small Bible college that sometimes had less than 30 students. His friends and family thought that he was being idiotic in maintaining that this place was the place where God had called him. To them, it was vocational suicide. Nevertheless, he persevered and later became a teacher there. At one point, as he and his wife started a new phase, they had a house and no students. One student came to be with them, but having seen that he was the only student, he quietly slipped out during the night. What a great beginning to the new phase. From the outside, it didn't seem as though he were making such great leadership decisions.

Sometimes people don't understand this way of living. Later in Oswald's life, he was dubbed by another missionary as the "apostle of the haphazard," because Oswald emphasized so strongly that we discover God's will through what he called "the haphazard circumstances of life." He was the antiplanner. He wrote to his wife, Biddy, these words in a letter: "I never see my way. I know God who guides so I fear nothing. I have never far-seeing plans, only confident trust."

In a deep way, Oswald saw some of the things that Christians practically plan as antithetical to what God wants to do. Their hard labor under these plans becomes blocks to what God is doing. He gave these thoughts to his Bible students:

> "The great enemy to the Lord Jesus Christ in the present day is the conception of practical work that has not come from the

New Testament, but from the systems of the world in which endless energy and activities are insisted upon, but no private life with God."

Chambers reflected on leadership in a different way. He thought of leadership in terms of a relationship with God. He said that you really know that things are happening when people don't even know that you are there. He spoke and wrote passionately about the importance of being in Christ, rather than planning some way of your own.

Chambers died while serving as a YMCA chaplain in Egypt. He was treasured by those around him, but few would have realized then the impact he would eventually have. His wife, Gertrude "Biddy" Chambers, is really the secret unleader in Oswald's story. She patiently printed up his sermons and lectures that would never have been known without her. She transcribed hundreds of pages of shorthand notes to get ready for the devotional sections of Chambers' work. She was the editor and compiler, making all the selections. It was three years of hard work, but in the end, she only put her initials, B. C. in the foreword of the book that became so amazingly popular. Her husband's name was on the front. She was the secret unleader who really influenced the world, and without her I would not be writing about Oswald. She was an incessant advocate of his writings, and now they have blessed the world.

As I was reading Chambers's biography, I ran into a man on the street who had been homeless. He had all kinds of challenges and difficulties. I noticed that he was clutching a book in his hand; it was a copy of *My Utmost for His Highest*. You never know the twists and turns in the effect of a man like Chambers who made such poor "career choices." He was one who told us not to make our own plans.

Our understanding of plans touches the deepest part of our lives. We are all going to have to trust something, whether it is ourselves, or our lover, or our money, or the chair we are sitting on. We are always in some kind of trusting relationship. Sometimes we forget that the word for *faith* and *trust* in the New Testament is the same word. This translation for both words makes sense to me.

When I first arrived in the Lower East Side, I felt as though I had entered a world like no other I had ever experienced. People lived in abandoned buildings. Acquaintances made alliances in order to survive. Villains with tire irons walked the streets—and they would use those tire irons. You would give money to someone, and they would betray you. Drugs were the mainstay of the economy, and putting faith in the wrong person could be deadly. The question I heard over and over again was this one: "Can I trust him?"

Who can I trust? This was the supreme question in a world where survival seemed questionable. Later, a friend of mine, who had gone through a horrible trauma with the one he loved, said afterward, "I learned that the question is not 'Why?' The question is 'Who?' Who can I trust in these difficult times?"

A discussion of plans points to the deepest questions in our life, and we should go carefully. The Bible says not only that we can trust God, but that God is working all things for good for those of us who love Him and are called according to His purposes (Romans 8:28). Trusting involves believing that a friend will follow through, even though it doesn't look as though the friend is doing so. Clearly, many times it doesn't look as though God can use all things for good. Yet it is very hard for a pawn to see the whole board. It is harder for my pet to understand how a rabies shot might in the end help him and others. It is even harder for the cat to understand algebra.

If faith and trust are the same word in the New Testament, we use "faith" every day. It is not some spooky mysterious religious thing. We use faith when we buy a cup of coffee and drink it, trusting that it is not poison. We use faith when we hand the newspaperman money for the newspaper. We both trust that money will be honored. We use faith when we walk into a building, trusting that the architect and structural engineer did a good job and the building will not collapse. We cannot avoid using faith. In the end, we are putting faith either in cosmic randomness, or in cosmic purpose. We just can't get away from faith. The world is too big for us.

Obedience and Tossing Your Hat over the Wall

*T*he Bible talks about a different way to live. " When you turn, whether to the right or to the left, your ears will hear a voice behind you saying this is the way, walk in it" (Isaiah 30:21). This is another way to make decisions. Or how would that man Ananias know that the instruction to go to the street called Straight would be perhaps the most important thing he ever did, that the address would lead him to a man named Saul, who would eventually be Paul, and who would write a large portion the New Testament (Acts 9:11).

Of course, getting guidance from God in the Bible involves responding to the guidance. We can't say, "Lord, show me what to do and I will consider it as one of my options in a menu of considerations." We get back to the logic of the possibility of God existing. If there really is a God, all-knowing, who holds time and space as a coin, so to speak, in His pocket, then it would be idiotic to treat Him like a fool. No, if we follow this path, we are saying that when You show me Your way and Your path, which is always the path of love, I am obedient. This path of love will be confirmed by the Word of God and usually by those Christian brothers and sisters closest to us.

I don't think we can ever get away from the fact that being obedient to God's plans is an act of faith. For example, I don't ever remember seeing a ministry implemented in obedience to God's plans where all the resources were there as the person started. Apparently with God, stepping out in trust and dependence without seeing the whole timetable of financial resourcing is part of His plan.

We have seen this so many times in stepping out in God's leading in our ministry in community service in New York City. If we made our own plans on the endeavor, I would say it could never be done. I read a story a long time ago about a writer who was hiking cross-country through England. He said that sometimes, since they weren't following the roads, they would encounter a wall or hedge so high that they could not scale it. He said that then, he would simply take off his hat and throw it over the wall. That way he knew that, one way or other, he would find a way to get over. I think that sometimes when we sense God's leading in a plan, confirmed by His Word, we have a moment of trepidation. What if things don't go right? What if we fail? What if we don't have enough resources? Those are the times when we need to whip off our hats (metaphorically speaking) and toss them over the wall. Take the first step out on the water, and trust the Planner to help us with the next one.

Stepping Out into Uncertainty

*I*sn't it amazing that the people of God in Exodus ate something called manna for 40 years? It appeared each day but on the day of rest. For 40 years they call this daily bread, this provision right when they need it, a name that means "What is it?" (Exodus 16). They never completely understood how it happened. How often do we take the provision for the day and have to say "What is it?" We don't understand either.

I remember a time when I first became a Christian and I had a sense that the plan I had made about going to law school was not the right one. I felt God's leading to go to seminary, but it didn't make sense to me. I didn't know what I would do afterward. I talked to my Christian friends. I spoke with wise counselors and professors. I read the Bible. You never know what will touch you. I was told a simple sentence from Dietrich Bonhoeffer—it was what spoke to me. He said something like this: "To be a Christian, you must step out into uncertainty." That was it. That was what I felt like. I had no real plan and I was stepping out into uncertainty. His sentence helped me do it. I didn't even realize then all the agonizing choices Bonhoeffer had to make to follow God in Nazi Germany.

After I went to seminary, my wife and I went as missionaries to Hong Kong. I was struck by the fact that even on a worldly level, set plans can be stultifying. I remember reading a story about a Chinese mandarin in some paper while I was there. A young soldier was contemplating marrying the woman that he loved, but marrying her was a terrible setback to his career plans. He would not be able to do what he planned to do. The mandarin listened quietly, and finally responded with this loaded statement—"The planned life can only be endured." It is true. Perhaps the worst thing that could happen would be for all our petty little plans to come true. What a rigid, joyless life, without the thousand surprises that our Lord provides when we follow Him.

Don't get me wrong. I don't intend to sound Pollyannaish or superficial about making plans. When the disciples began to follow Jesus, do you really think that they knew what they were getting into? Did they understand that practically all of them would eventually be killed because they followed Him? Did they anticipate the healings, the feeding of thousands, the power of their own preaching and casting out demons? Did they anticipate the fear and betrayal and torture of their leader? I doubt it. But in the end, would any of them sincerely have wished to have done anything else with their life? Would they have wished that they hadn't followed Him? I doubt it.

There is a way to live that seems to defy our plans and gives a different kind of life to each day. "The wind blows where it wishes, and you hear its sound, but you do not know where it comes from or where it goes," Jesus says to Nicodemus, a man who is at the time still thinking through the obstetric challenges of being born again. Jesus continues, "So it is with everyone who is born of the Spirit" (John 3:8). This is another way of seeing the world.

The Secret Stair

*G*eorge MacDonald is a person who thought long and hard about the way of God and how to live that. He had his own experiences as a failure in preaching in the nineteenth century, and at times had to live with a certain amount of shame and humiliation. He wrote a poem that typifies this other way to live:

THE HOLY THING

THEY all were looking for a king
To slay their foes and lift them high:
Thou cam'st, a little baby thing
That made a woman cry.

Our plans seem to make a lot of sense to us, with kings and power and all. The Christian story is a story of another plan. The poem goes on.

O Son of Man, to right my lot
Naught but Thy presence can avail;
Yet on the road Thy wheels are not,
Nor on the sea Thy sail!

When a leader is so intent on his own plan, he ends up in huff with God. Our prayers become a profound disappointment. We look for help in our way, yet on the road we don't see God's "wheels." And we keep waiting for our ship to come in, but it never seems to. But here is the clincher.

My how or when Thou wilt not heed,
But come down Thine own secret stair,
That Thou mayst answer all my need —
Yea, every bygone prayer.

Our plans almost always seem so architecturally sound to us. But God does not heed them. He has his own "secret stair." I imagine the grand stairway in the front, where everyone is expecting the majestic entrance. I can see the tiny little staircase in the back that no one knows about. Isn't that just like Jesus? He still keeps appearing in a cradle instead of a palace. I have to be careful with this poem I love so much. Once I preached a sermon on it, and a woman in the back told me she thought I was talking about the Lord's secret *stare* during the entire service. Oh, well. But unless we understand that God has His own secret way of doing things, our leadership may end up in frustration or despair. To follow this path, we live in a plan-less plan, that requires faithfulness, loyalty, and a touch of panache.

principle #4
Think Small

Nothing is so small but God is still smaller, nothing is so large but God is still larger, nothing is so short but God is still shorter, nothing so long but God is still longer, nothing is so broad, but God is still broader, nothing so narrow but God is still narrower.

Martin Luther

The Little Way

Big doesn't mean strong and small doesn't mean weak. This walk in the Spirit always carries two truths from the Scriptures. One truth comes from Zechariah 4:10. The people were working to rebuild the temple, and they had gotten discouraged at the delays. It seems as though the people were inferring that the temple they were working on was not as grand and magnificent as the one Solomon had built before them, the one that had been destroyed. They had gotten into that classic mental trap of saying that things were not as good as they were in the old days. God speaks to the people a word of encouragement, and tells us them not to despise "the day of small things." In our work in the Lower East Side, we have taken this Scripture and talked about the ministry of small things, of doing the little thing with great love and refusing to denigrate it.

The other truth comes from Ephesians 3:17–19. This letter comes from a man in jail, a man who is probably facing execution, and yet he is so excited about what God is doing through Christ, he can hardly contain himself. Paul has had some rough times, but he reminds us that as we are rooted and grounded in love, that we can comprehend the heights and depths. Ultimately we will know the love of Christ, and he uses the astonishing phrase that we "may be filled with the fullness of God." Amazing! He then reminds us that God can do far more than we can ask or think. What a stretching, mind-blowing, vision-expanding statement. We know that we can think of a lot of things, but God can do more.

Here are the two truths that we carry side by side, like a principle and an antiprinciple, like matter and antimatter. One Scripture reminds us that God works through small things. The other Scripture reminds us that God can do far more than we could think of or even imagine. We should carry both truths in our pocket, or perhaps both truths should carry us. God's work extends beyond the farthest things we can imagine, as well as within the smallest things we can conceive. His influence reaches farther than the vast expanse of universes and deeper than a quark — the smallest particle of an atom.

Throughout human history, someone has always talked about "the little way." Therese of Lisieux in the nineteenth century was one of them. Even though she died when she was only 24 years old, she touched the world by showing people a different way in her letters and writings. This little way is to seek out the menial job and befriend the ungrateful person. Therese talked about doing the smallest act for God. We choose the little things in life to show God's greatness:

> "The most trivial act, one that no one knows about, provided it is inspired by love, is often of greater worth than the greatest achievement. It is not the value or even apparent holiness of deeds which counts, but only the love put into them. And no one can say he cannot do these little things for God, for everyone is capable of them."

There is a power that comes when a person isn't afraid of the little way. You can see the peace in them regardless of what they are doing. When everything is done for the love of God, instead of for some other agenda, it really doesn't matter what a person is doing. This way of going about things turns our normal notions on their head. I often resist the little way. However, I have always been interested in watching the path of some high-powered CEOs of major companies in New York City. I've seen a few who have worked vastly stressful jobs for 60 hours a week or more in order to attain a goal. And what is their goal? To retire early and live in a house back in the woods. And what do they want to do there? Simple things, like chop wood and push a wheelbarrow around and garden. Go figure. Maybe they should have just worked for a landscaper at the beginning, and they could have been pushing that wheelbarrow a lot earlier. There is something in us that longs for the simple things, and something in us that resists this.

This little way is very hard for some leaders. Make no small plans, we are instructed, for large plans and visions draw the best out of people. These instructions are sometimes true, and I suppose they should be remembered. But the fact of the matter is, God chooses little things so often that we really can't ignore them.

For me, Elisha is one of the masters of the little way. His leader and mentor, Elijah, was quite a dramatic fellow. Elijah strides across the stage of human history with his outlandish clothes and immediately calls down a drought upon the land. He faces off against an evil king, has a showdown with the prophets of Baal, and runs a full marathon in the rain (1 Kings 17-19). Elijah calls down fire on soldiers that come to arrest him, and even his departure from earth is dramatic as he goes up in a whirlwind with chariots of fire and horses of fire. He is a hard act to follow.

The only thing we know that Elisha did after Elijah had called him was that he "poured water on the hands of Elijah" (2 Kings 3:11). In contrast to Elijah's first act on the scene, who proclaimed a drought on the land, Elisha quietly put salt on a stream and made it drinkable again. Elisha helps a widow who is in debt, and restores the only son of an older woman. He purifies a deadly stew. He recovers an axe head. Naaman, the Syrian general, gets angry at Elisha because Elisha doesn't ask the general to do anything dramatic or stupendous in order to be healed. The general needs only to wash himself seven times in the relatively little Jordan River. Elisha does his small acts of kindness in a small way, in contrast to his dramatic predecessor (2 Kings 2–7). But these quiet acts have a huge impact on the people who are the recipients.

Sometimes the little way is important because it keeps the helper from being overwhelmed. Trying to do everything at once may make a leader feel important, but sometimes such an approach ends up achieving little. Many times I have watched the person at the information booth at Grand Central Station. Sometimes there is a crowd of people, all in a hurry to catch their train, shouting out questions and needing immediate answers. Sometimes they don't even stand in line. I love the way the person at the desk will calmly look one person in the eyes, understand her question, and give an answer. Then the information person will calmly turn to the next questioner, so that information can be given directly and efficiently. The information person can't answer them all at once. That would be the big way. Instead, he or she chooses a focused approach. It looks like a littler way.

As we read the Bible more deeply, we find that we get more than just factual information. What we find is that our own center of consciousness begins to touch another, larger center of consciousness. It is a quieting thought to realize that the One who made the unique and amazing personalities we have is not just a force. God has personality too. I think that as we read the Word of God, that personality emerges.

I do not say this disrespectfully, but I believe there is a quirk in God's personality. Here it is—He loves to take small things and make great things out of them. He will take the staff of a shepherd and make it the rod that helps liberate a people. He will take a young boy with five stones to kill the giant oppressor of Israel. He will take a little boy's lunch and feed thousands. To put it colloquially, God gets a kick out of doing things this way. That should be, I think, an encouragement for us unleaders. We are little, too, and our resources may be small. Hooray! This is just the kind of situation God enjoys.

Preaching to Thousands

A refusal to think small can lead to great things, but sometimes it can block what God is doing. I can remember very well a talented man who came to our ministry in the early days. He told me that God had given him a vision that he was going to preach to thousands. I said, "That is great! How about starting by talking to that gentleman over there sitting on the park bench? He really needs someone who would spend some time with him."

The man looked disappointed and shook his head. "But God has called me to preach to thousands."

I told him, "That is wonderful! Every journey starts with one step. How about sharing the good news of your experience with that fellow on the park bench? The best part of preaching is sharing that good news." We talked many times. The man stayed around for a while but never took the first steps, finally drifting away, getting involved with something else. I'm not sure he was ever able to preach to thousands.

On the other hand, we had another young man who came to our ministry. We told him the only thing we had for him to do was work with the children. It wasn't his final aim, but he did it. Later he washed pots and pans for our meal for the homeless for two years. He never once complained, but did just what he was asked to do. Now he does preach at a church in Manhattan, and he probably preaches to over a thousand a week. He didn't let the small things stop him.

It is hard to see in foresight what small thing may have a huge impact. It is easy to track these things in hindsight. Barclay's commentary tells a story of a monk in the fourth century who felt impelled to leave his desert prayers and go to the city. The monk came to Rome as they were celebrating a victory over the Goths. The monk found his way to the gladiator games. He didn't go with a plan to change the world. However, he was so aghast at the violence and gratuitous injuries he saw there that he actually got into the arena himself. He stood between the gladiators. The crowd was furious that he had interrupted their afternoon entertainment and threw stones at him. Eventually a gladiator drew his sword and killed the monk. As the monk crumpled to the ground, the entire crowd became silent. They left the arena with a hushed tone. The gladiator games were never resumed in Rome, because of the one man of prayer and his action at one event.

Sometimes people who are accustomed to having a huge impact have to think small. After his many military victories, David was accustomed to having people acknowledge that "David killed his ten thousands." He had big plans for the temple, big plans for battles, big plans for the kingdom. When we read the lyrics of his songs, we see that he was confident that God delighted in him.

Yet when he committed immorality with another man's wife, and lied and schemed about it, and maneuvered a murder, he had to think small again. No longer could he think about his kingdom, or his subjects, or his soldiers. He had to think about his own heart. David was accustomed to making huge and kingly sacrifices to God. But in his song of repentance for what he had done, he said this:

> "For you would not delight in sacrifice, or I would give it; you will not be pleased with a burnt offering. The sacrifices of God are a broken spirit; a broken and contrite heart, O God, you will not despise" (Psalm 51:16–17).

David had to move away from all his great victory battles, his love conquests, his desire to make royal sacrifices to God. He couldn't bring a proud, pumped-up leader's heart. He had to narrow things down to his own broken and contrite heart. He had to think that small.

The Shrinking of Vision

*W*ith the expansion of vision in the Bible, there is also a shrinking of vision. God gets so scandalously particular in choosing just one person—Abraham, in order to bless all nations of the world. As we mentioned, God keeps leading down to smaller things, the staff of Moses, the five stones of David, the little boy's loaves and the fishes, all these little things that lead to things that greatly affect us.

We just have to mention the story of Gideon. What an unleader. We first find him hiding in a winepress threshing wheat. Threshing wheat involves letting the wind take away the chaff. That doesn't work so well when you are hiding in a winepress. The season of threshing was hot. Gideon was probably frustrated trying to make something work without wind, concealing himself from his enemies, and you can tell as the angel of the Lord appears to him.

When the angel says, "The Lord is with you, O mighty man of valor," you can almost hear Gideon saying, "Are you crazy?" Instead, Gideon asks, if the Lord is with us, then why have all these terrible things happened to us? He furthers his challenge by asking where are all the miracles that happened back in the day? As the conversation continues, he asserts that his is the weakest clan and he is the least of his family. He wasn't exactly the natural leader leaping to the forefront.

Once he finally gathers a group to fight the Midianites (their enemies), God starts shrinking the resources. First, it seems that Gideon has 32,000 men and God tells him to release 22,000. Then God says there are still too many. All but 300 were released. God has to encourage Gideon again. Gideon probably first looked at the 300 and then at the number of Midianites and felt as though his 300 were dead men walking. God had to buck up Gideon's courage by helping him overhear the enemy. The victory was won, but sometimes in the process God makes His own people less and less rather than more and more (Judges 6–8).

Jesus had to deal with the shrinking of the number of people following Him too. After He fed the five thousand, He had to say some hard things, and the Bible says that many of the disciples turned back and no longer walked with Him. It seems as though so many people left, Jesus had to even ask the disciples if they were planning to bail also (John 6:66–67).

A few generations ago, Clarence Jordan was a man whose way seemed to get smaller and smaller. He was a farmer and a Greek scholar working in Georgia. He translated the New Testament. He had a sense of humor. The people in his community worked hard to follow the Sermon on the Mount by sharing their goods and including everyone from all races. In the 1950s in rural Georgia, the racial inclusion was particularly tough stuff. People said that hanging around the people that were drawn to him made Jordan a communist. He said, "Being around those people doesn't any more make me a communist than being around you makes me an idiot."

A preacher was so proud when he showed him the new cross on the front of his building that cost many thousands of dollars. "Friend, you got cheated," Jordan said. "There was a time when you could have gotten one of those for free."

His group was shot at, their goods were boycotted, and he was thrown out of the local Baptist church. Years went on, and the idealistic people in his own community got worn out, and one by one they drifted away. Eventually, there were only two families left—Clarence's family and another family. The community was clearly at an end, and Clarence was discouraged. He had had a great vision, but the reality had actually gotten smaller and smaller, down to two families. He planned to sell the property. During this period, a young man and his wife had chanced to come by the community. The young man was unusual. He had already earned a million dollars and had given it away and was praying about what to do next. He had reached a crisis of faith.

He and Clarence talked about the ideas in the Bible and the fact that people didn't need charity but capital. They dreamed of a Fund for Humanity.

Clarence died not too long afterward. From some perspectives, his endeavors looked like a failure. The local officials would not even come out to proclaim that Clarence was dead. His dead body had to be loaded into a station wagon by the young man and taken in. That young man who had dreamed with him stayed for a while and then moved on with his life. His name was Millard Fuller. The seed had been planted. He eventually started the organization partially based on their discussions—Habitat for Humanity. As Fuller helped the organization expand into a hundred countries, he has had his own challenges. Still, it is clear that Habitat for Humanity would not be here without Jordan's shrinking community. After Jordan's death, his community in Georgia also experienced a rebirth.

"Unless a grain of wheat falls into the earth and dies, it remains alone; but if it dies, it brings forth much fruit" (John 12:12). Jesus helped us see the pattern, but you never know when something might be in the dying stage just before it is going to be reborn. The despair that Clarence felt as he watched his community shrink was a real despair. It gives a leader pause.

Jim Cymbala talks about coming to pastor a church that only had a handful of people. The church seemed like a spiritual and financial mess. He and his wife, Carol, took on the responsibilities of providing shepherding for this group. As they worked, they noticed that the number of people attending had dropped—to about 20. As he continued, at one point he says that he began to pray that certain people would leave. Some he had to confront and suggest that they find another church. It was a hard time. One Sunday night, he was at his lowest point. He told the group that he could no longer preach and, as his wife played, he leaned on the pulpit, sobbing. The group crowded around him and prayed for help. A spirit of intercession came upon them, and the usher came up weeping and confessed to stealing some of the offering.

Cymbala said that in the time of prayer, Problem Number One, out of seemingly thousands, was solved. He further realized, there at that low moment, that "God is attracted to weakness. He can't resist those who humbly and honestly admit how desperately they need Him. Our weakness, in fact, makes room for His power." It was almost as if God had to shrink Cymbala's resources and vision in order for the ministry to grow and touch so many others in the way it has. But at that time of difficulty, it would have been hard to see what the church would become and the blessing it would be to the nation.

We study the letters of Corinth, and think of them as some of the most profound pieces ever written. They are quoted and emblazoned around the world. I was surprised to read the archaeological evidence of the size of the church Paul was writing to. There were a bunch of cell groups, and they all met in the house of a rich man in Corinth. The archaeologists tell us that a wealthy man's house could only hold about 50 people. Think of the time Paul poured into the limited number of people there.

We often say in churches that where two or more are gathered together, there will Christ be. However, Jesus actually says, "where two or three" are gathered together. Why do we keep changing the words of Jesus? In a novella by Will Campbell, the three Christians who are being hunted discuss the reason for this limit in the Scriptures. One of the Christians says, "Because when there are more than two or three, they start looking for a leader. He's in the midst of two or three but not four or five or eight hundred." Is it possible that some leader's big plans can get in the way of what God is doing?

You Can't Be Too Small for God to Use

Sometimes one doesn't even have two or three gathered together. I've often read about a man who loved Jesus and whose life helped many people in the last 100 years. Communities of Christians have been influenced by him all over the world. His name is Charles de Foucauld. He was a military man and had many adventures. However, as he grew older, he was gripped with the power of the simplicity of Jesus. He began to feel that instead of adding more and more religious trappings we should add less and less. He wanted to connect with people who were like his Master, a carpenter's son. He learned that one is approachable in helping others not because one is so big, but because one is so small.

In his prayers and his reflections and his writing, he showed that he was thinking smaller and smaller. His journey took him to northern Africa where he was in a simple, secluded space with hopes of starting a community there. He seemed to think very small instead of thinking very big. He said, "What I dream of is something very plain and few in number, similar to the little communities of the first Christians . . . living the life of Nazareth, through work and the contemplation of Jesus . . . a little family, a little home, very small, very plain." Through some strange twists and turns, he was murdered by robbers. At the time of his death in North Africa, he did not have one companion or follower with him. He was all alone. From anyone's perspective, Charles's role as a leader at the time of his death seemed like a failure. Of course, there was a Saturday after Jesus' death when His life and goals looked like a failure too. It is hard to see on that Saturday what was to come afterward.

It may be a cut to the pride to think of doing things in a small way. But this way can also help us learn to listen in a new way, and understand better the saying that you can't be too small for God to use, only too big.

principle #5
Associate with Losers

A Wounded Deer — leaps highest

Emily Dickinson

The Danger of Being Successful

*T*here is great wisdom for leaders to talk about associating with successful people. It is good practical advice spiritually also. "Whoever walks with the wise becomes wise" as the Proverb says (13:20). We might as well learn how to do a thing well, rather than the thousand ways to do a thing wrong. We associate with the wise and the successful and we learn. Besides, being with the wise and the successful helps us to be mentored by them, and perhaps they can assist us in the connections that are so important in life.

Yet an inner common sense tells us that associating only with successful people can be dangerous. It is hard to describe, but we know it inside. We can lose a sense of what living is, and at worst can become callous to the deeper workings of life. All of us have seen temporarily successful people who begin to think that they know more than they do. It is a blindness to be avoided.

For me, Sherwood Anderson said it best in 1927. He wrote a wonderful article about visiting Herbert Hoover before he became president. According to Anderson, Herbert Hoover was a very competent and successful man. He lived in a world of crisp goals and achievable objectives, and he had been very good at achieving his goals. Anderson continued:

> "He is, apparently, a man very sure of himself. His career has been a notable one. From a small beginning he has risen steadily in power. There has never been any check. I felt, looking at him, that he has never known failure."

Then Anderson, as a journalist who was interviewing the prospective next president, made this comment about knowing failure: "It is too bad never to have known that. Never to have known miserable nights of remorse, feeling the world too big and strange and difficult for you."

The article took on deeper meaning as Hoover became president of the United States and eventually presided over the Wall Street crash and Black Friday as the nation moved into the Great Depression. The sense of fear and malaise hovered over the country, and Hoover did not seem to be able to do much about it.

Polio and Depression

Franklin Roosevelt, the following president, had a different journey. He was also very successful in everything he did, and had the brightest of futures. One day, after many outdoor activities, he went to bed early because he didn't feel well. He never walked properly again.

Roosevelt took a number of paths to deal with what was then diagnosed as polio. He bought a spa to administer water therapy for himself and others. For a while he was deeply depressed. People diagnosed with polio at that time often resigned themselves to a wheelchair and a reclusive life. Roosevelt exercised and wore a brace so that he looked as though he could walk again. Perhaps spending time with others who had polio helped his own political views to mature, and gave him a different appreciation of the difficulties of others.

He ran for governor of New York State and then for president. He would follow Herbert Hoover as president. As he entered office, a tangible change could be felt in the country. "There is nothing to fear but fear itself," he said. He embarked on the hundred days of innovation and experimentation that changed our country. He had the right combination of warmth, understanding, and determination that was able to help those across the country pick up where they left off and carry on. I wonder if part of that quality didn't come from spending time with people in wheelchairs and with people wearing braces. In addition to everything that happened under Roosevelt's leadership, we can't forget his energy in helping begin the foundation (eventually called the March of Dimes) that provided the funds to produce the successful polio vaccine. One wonders if Roosevelt could possibly have foreseen all that would happen in the midst of his own personal depression in the 1920s.

It is clear that associating with winners has many advantages. But association with losers gives one a new kind of ears. People who work with the homeless cannot walk the streets in the same way. The issue stops being about homelessness; it starts to be about John or Sarah or José. There is a distinct danger when everything in life works well for a person. It can separate the winners from the losers in a wrong way. It creates a temporary illusion for winners that will probably not last, an illusion that we ourselves are able to manage things. On the other hand, something happens when life seems bigger than we can handle because--guess what? In reality, it is.

Another Lame Man

No one seemed to have a more promising career than Albert Schweitzer. Still in his twenties, he wrote a book on the quest for the historical Jesus that is still read by seminary students today. He was a wonderful performer of Bach on the organ, and he had written a book on the proper maintenance of organs that played Bach. He was a very young man when he became the equivalent of a dean of a divinity school in Germany.

Still something had been working on him. He saw an invitation to help in Africa in a missions magazine. He closed the magazine and felt a great peace. He knew what he was to do. He would go to medical school and become a doctor and work with those who needed help the most.

The interesting thing to me is the reaction of his friends. Few were encouraging, in light of his brilliant future academic and cultural career. One person told him that it was like sending a general to do a private's work. With his training, he would be intellectually thwarted by going to a poor and illiterate place in the Congo. Most of Schweitzer's friends felt that going there would be a life of stagnation tantamount to a death sentence. Also, his theology was unorthodox and his views were extremely different from the conservative missionary group that he applied to.

Still, Schweitzer went. He unpacked one of his wooden crates and made a table out of it, and used that desk for his intellectual work. He practiced the organ on a fake keyboard. He built a hospital and later a community for lepers. In the middle of a very poor community, he continued to do surgery, continued to administer medicine, continued to think about life, continued to write books, and continued his work with Bach and organ music. People say that for 50 years, he had only one formal suit to wear at concerts or other special events.

His life seemed to be culturally separated from his European background, and yet he has influenced more people than anyone ever expected, and perhaps for more good. We can argue all day about his theology and his political sensibilities, but his practical acts pointed to a different way.

Here is an example of how associating with losers can help. For a time, during World War I, Schweitzer and his wife were imprisoned. They were both very sick. Eventually they were released and were in the process of making some urgent and timely train changes when Schweitzer found that he was too weak to carry his suitcase. People passed him by, not realizing his desperate need. A kind person, who was lame himself, came to Schweitzer's aid. Schweitzer was deeply moved. He made the commitment that whenever he saw a person needing help with a suitcase, he would help. His association with the others in prison, the lack of his usual robust health, and one lame person had changed him.

The effects of these experiences continued to change him. One time Schweitzer came to Chicago to perform Bach selections in order to raise money for his hospital. By this time, his work in Africa had become well known. When he arrived on the train, reporters were there to greet Dr. Albert Schweitzer and get a story. They crowded around him, but before he answered their questions, he stopped and helped an older woman carry her suitcase to the train. The younger people there, with their thoughts on their story, took a moment to think about why they hadn't even noticed the woman. Perhaps the younger ones had never had trouble carrying a suitcase at a station. But then, Schweitzer always did see things a little upside down. He'd been one who was sick and trying to catch an extremely important train that took him to freedom. He saw that the healthy successful ones at that earlier station had not seen him. A man who was crippled himself did.

Pigeonholing and the Nature of Love

*W*hy was it so important that Jesus gave instructions on how to have a party or a banquet? He said that we were to invite the poor, the maimed, the lame, and the blind (Luke 14:13–14). What was so important about spending time with this group? It's easy to talk about doing this, or maybe to do it once a year on the day before Thanksgiving. But it can be tough to do day in and day out—the smells, the sores, the dirt. You know what I mean. Why did Jesus give here such specific instructions for the company we keep? He says that we should do it because they cannot pay us back. For once it isn't a business meal. For once it isn't a family meal with relatives to whom it is their due. For once it isn't a meal to enhance your social standing. For once, there isn't another agenda. For once you don't have to fit people in any pay-back category whatsoever.

The developmental stage that classifies people into winners and losers should probably end in middle school. (It didn't for me.) A woman in our ministry shared this thought—whenever you pigeonhole someone, you cease to love them. You close off the possibilities of what they are and what they are to become. Here is a little bit of her story. She did not like the young people who roam around in our area. They often seem unwashed. They use heroin and other drugs in the park. They have scruffy, dirty dogs with them. They beg on the street even though they are able-bodied. They currently call themselves "travelers." Some people call them crusty punks. She was a hairstylist and found these "travelers" distasteful.

One day she noticed that a group of travelers were camping out in a parked car right outside her hairstyling shop. It was New York, and she really couldn't do anything about it. In spite of herself, as she styled hair, she had an opportunity to watch how they lived for three days. What struck her most was the care and love they gave to their dogs. She had her own dogs and loved them. Something began to happen to her heart.

She said she wanted to reach out to the dogs of this group and through care for their dogs to reach out to the travelers themselves. To me, this particular group was very anti-authoritarian and rarely gave me the time of day without a curse to go along with it. They are, from my view, also very tribal and committed to being with people that looked and acted like they did. I told the woman that she could use the front of our building, but that it would take a long time to reach out to them.

The first night she offered dog biscuits and vegetarian sandwiches. About 20 travelers were sitting on the sidewalk in front of our ministry with their dogs. I couldn't believe it. Her work with this group has exploded, with a vast network of people taking care of the dogs and befriending the travelers, wherever they roam. She calls the work "Collide" because it is where two cultures — hers and theirs — collide. Contact has been made, walls are broken down, and the pigeonholing has started to fade.

Last month I got up early to walk along the East River and pray. It was very early in the morning and the section of the walk felt a little dicey when no one but me was there. A group of seven young men approached me, and they all had that strut that tough young men sometimes have when they are in a group. They were travelers, and it looked as though they had been up all night and were looking for some last bit of trouble. The first one was a big one. We were all aware that there was one of me and seven of them.

"Got money?" the big one asked with a mocking sneer.

"Nope," I said and walked past them, probably with my own little stance.

Each one passed me, and leaned toward me with just a hint of intimidation, since we were all alone there in the early morning. A few had their thumbs in their belts. The last one that passed looked at me, and his hard face broke into a grin. "Hey!"

he shouted, "Good to see you!" He had been at Collide in front of our building the night before. I called out his name. The mood of the whole group changed entirely. "You going for a run?" my friend from the night before asked.

"No, just a prayerwalk," I called back cheerily. We could have been suburbanites exchanging pleasantries as we watered our lawns. My whole view of the group changed. This I have seen many times. This one woman's heart to stop pigeonholing will eventually affect people and times she would have never imagined. It affected me.

Strength in Weakness

The change from pigeonholing winners and losers started for me in a storefront many years ago. We had a Bible study for people in our tough neighborhood. Anyone was welcome, and people floated in and out from the street. I remembered attending a therapy group in another city focusing particularly on mentally ill patients. They called the group "Winner's Circle." In my own mind, I had dubbed this group in the storefront as "Loser's Circle." On some nights, the people seemed worse than mentally ill. They were violent, deranged, alcoholic, deaf, incoherent, criminal, out of control.

Louisa was a young woman who attended regularly. She insisted on reading the Scripture. This was a problem for me, because her speech impediment kept anyone from understanding at all what was read. But she was unabashed and unstoppable. She read with sincere passion and absolutely no one could understand what she read. Yet somehow, when she read, the entire group calmed down. They got quiet in a way that they didn't when others read. Perhaps it was the steady conviction she exuded to all that what she was doing had value for them. They listened, and then they began to speak more softly to each other as they interacted. Her reading somehow kept the group together.

On one tedious night, she was reading about weakness and she could barely stumble through the words. The Scripture was written by that unleader Paul. It was about being made perfect in weakness. Everyone was particularly silent, and I finally realized that I myself would be a lesser person if I didn't come to "Loser's Circle." In some nonconceptual, nonverbal way, she gave something to us that I couldn't have received in another more fast-paced, competent group. Any leaders, who tried to streamline their lives by eliminating their contact with someone like Louisa, would have truly been the losers.

principle #6
Get Off the Cutting Edge

Even in literature and art, no man who bothers about originality will ever be original: whereas if you simply try to tell the truth (without caring twopence how often it has been told before) you will, nine times out of ten, become original without ever having noticed it.

C. S. Lewis in *Mere Christianity*

When Relevancy Becomes Irrelevant

*P*eople have almost always talked about how fast things are changing. This language of rapid transition is not necessarily new language. You can read the same kind of talk in ancient literature. We might as well stop whining about the rapid changes. So much of leadership material talks about keeping up with the times and being ahead of the curve. When we read this kind of writing, it sometimes feels as though we must always battle to be just ahead of some cresting wave. Sometimes we just feel a little bit left behind and maybe just a little tired of paddling so urgently.

But in reality, we are not trying to locate what is the latest thing. In fact, there may be things more important than being ahead of the curve. Rather, we are looking toward what is true. "Current" is not necessarily the same as true. Many people now think our society has moved to a place where we can't ever really know if anything is true. Again, this is not a new perspective. A couple of thousand years ago, Pilate asked with a world-weary sophistication, "What is truth?" (John 18:38).

It would be a sad thing to judge people by how "relevant" their work is. Putting our energies toward what is relevant can really become a distraction. Eugene Peterson, the pastor and translator, makes the wonderful comment that "if you dig your wells deep enough, relevancy is pretty much irrelevant."

Working to always keep up with the latest trend is very important on one level. But on another level, such a preoccupation can lead to a second-rate experience of life. The results are wasted time on things that aren't so important, an unhealthy penchant for fashion rather than substance, and a heart that is frittered away on getting the approval of people at the moment.

The Minister Who Lost His Way

*T*homas Merton wrote many books on prayer and meditation, but his life did not start out heading in that direction. In his biography, *The Seven Storey Mountain*, he has a telling story for me as a Protestant. As a young man, he was spiritually restless and searching for something. He loved avant-garde reading and jazz and the latest intellectual discussions. He was not a believer, but he was seeking. In his search, someone recommended a Protestant minister in Manhattan who was up-to-date and contemporary.

Merton went to meet him. The minister was congenial and conversant about a number of things that were important to Merton. However, in the end, Merton felt like the literature the minister talked about was not quite as up-to-date as his faster and younger friends. Trying to be contemporary, the minister was even a little behind the times. And nothing is quite so yesterday as *almost* current thoughts. Merton said that the minister maintained contact with people by reading the latest books. "He did not like or understand what was considered most 'advanced' in modern literature," Merton wrote, yet

> "it was modern literature and politics that he talked about, not religion and God. You felt that the man did not know his vocation, did not know what he was supposed to be. He had taken upon himself some function in society which was not his and which was, indeed, not a necessary function at all."

This experience was contrasted to talking to a priest. The priest didn't pretend to know the latest literature. He was not even trying to be up-to-date or relevant. What the priest talked about, however, were eternal truths. Truths that transcended the limits of our culture and time. Merton, in his circles, had rarely heard anyone talk like that. These conversations touched something deep within his heart, in a way very different from the Protestant pastor's attempts to make connections.

The rest is history. Merton became a Catholic and eventually a Cistercian monk.

The poet Robert Frost made a comment years ago that seems even truer today—"It may come to the notice of posterity . . . that this, our age, ran wild in the quest of new ways to be new." Whatever seems so new today will not seem so tomorrow, and a person who chases these new things may look back on a wasted life of timely mediocrity. This kind of language is not unfamiliar to Christians, and it is not really unique to our age. We remember the account in Acts where "all the Athenians and the foreigners who lived there would spend their time in nothing except telling or hearing something new" (17:21).

The Futility of Trying to Know It All

*W*e go through a stage sometimes when we think "the cutting edge" is extremely important. But often we go through other stages. Before I was a Christian, I read a lot about a novelist, Thomas Wolfe, who wrote some huge novels in the earlier part of the twentieth century. Thomas Wolfe was a southerner who came to New York City. At six-foot, seven inches tall, he wanted to experience everything in the city. He would walk the streets for hours and hours without stopping, just watching people. He was also a voracious reader. At one point in his life, he wanted to read everything in the Harvard Library. There are stories of Wolfe with a stop watch in the library, timing how fast he was reading a book, trying to get the main idea. By the end of his time in Boston, he had read a good chunk of the library's holdings. Perhaps it made him feel as though he were more attuned to the world he lived in.

But Wolfe came to a phase in his life where he ceased to try to read everything and ceased reading the current literature or trends. He quit trying to read the whole library and catch up on everything. He just kept a few books by his bedside and read those books more deeply. He was looking for the great writings, the things that struck deep in his heart, not just the endless flow of current material. Perhaps sometimes we need to think and read more slowly, as Wolfe did, rather than always finding ways to access more information more quickly and efficiently.

Certainly there is nothing wrong with keeping abreast of things. But the focus of the upside-down leader can get sidetracked by this chimera of keeping up. Ralph Waldo Emerson writes in his journal about doing something well, or better, or having something of quality, and the world will beat a path to your door, even if you live in the woods. This is the focus for the upside-down leader—doing something well, whether the thing is large or small. It doesn't matter whether you are in a big public forum or in the woods somewhere. Chasing after fashion, or public venues, or contemporary approval can bring some immediate success, but in the end, it leads to a superficial kind of experience.

Nassim Nicholas Taleb, the theorist on randomness mentioned in Principle #1, has some interesting things to say about working to keep up with the latest information. As a former financial trader, such information was held at a premium in his circles. But he challenges us to consider whether so much information is of dubious value. He talks about his grandfather, who served in positions of power in his home country, but who in reality really didn't know what was going to happen next. But he was the expert and had lots of knowledge at his fingertips. On the other hand, the driver for Taleb's grandfather knew he didn't know anything, and he simply said, "God knows," as his main commentary on events.

Taleb's position was that the driver was not an expert on these events and he knew it. The elite thinkers, on the other hand, thought they knew more than the non-elite, when in actuality they really didn't. In this situation, more and more information was not helpful. It may make you feel that you are becoming an expert, when you are really knowing less and less. He saw many newspapers, with their repetitive overlap, as an example of this kind of problem. A person works hard to stay on the cutting edge, reading all the latest articles, but in reality deludes himself into thinking that he knows more than he does.

My wife and I can relate to Taleb's comments. We both are avid news watchers, listening to the radio, watching the news on TV, reading thoughtful newspapers. We hang on to the latest news on the country's finances; we groan at the latest congressional foul-up. We've been guilty of interrupting time with company so that we can see some urgent update on TV. If we are not careful, we could become news monkeys.

But we have noticed something when we take a vacation. Sometimes we stay in a cabin up in the mountains. Our TV there is broken. The Christian station available in the mountains doesn't give the news. We seem to calm down as we are there. The opinions of popular commentators seem less and less important. We sometimes find that, after a few days, we are able to think more deeply about more important things, rather than about the latest political scandal or the latest famous person who had to go to rehab. When we return from the mountains, we can simply read a summary of the events. We often get a better perspective than if we had hung on to every word of the flash updates.

When we try to stay on the cutting edge of information, the problem is not in the acquiring of more information. The danger can come when we begin to think that we can necessarily understand things better than others, since we have had more access to sometimes repetitive or trivial information. It can become another kind of subtle pride where we delude ourselves that we know something when we don't. Maybe that kind of delusional confidence is one reason the Bible instructs us to "be not wise in your own eyes" (Proverbs 3:7).

Reading something from another time can help us have a new perspective that escapes us if we only consume "cutting edge" material. Marcus Aurelius, as an ancient Roman ruler, lived through some challenging times in an affluent society that had the leisure to take seriously the changing fashions. In stepping back and reflecting on life, he said that the object of life is not to be on the side of the majority, but to escape finding oneself in the ranks of the insane. Really now, if we stop to reflect, so much of our society is moving toward the bizarre and abnormal, merely because it is unusual and different, especially in the realms of violence and sexual exploitation. Eventually, finding the bizarre and the abnormal becomes an end in itself. Then we find that we ourselves are becoming more and more bizarre and off-the-track. But if we step off the merry-go-round for a bit and think about things more deeply and slowly, much of what is happening does look as though it is insane. We need to reverse things.

Stopping, or slowing down, is a key element for an unleader. When things are going quickly, we get caught up in the race, and we begin to think about what is up-to-speed rather than what is right or true. If we frame our life in terms of trying to be too much on the cutting edge, we could end up getting cut.

The Upside-down Satan

I had a seminary professor long ago that said that I would learn more theology from reading Dorothy Sayers's footnotes to Dante's *Divine Comedy* than I would learn from three years at the seminary. Once you get past all the gory details of Dante's *Inferno*, there is a portrayal of heaven and hell that I have never quite forgotten.

The story starts with Dante and his guide Virgil going into hell. As one descends into hell, one finds that, in some sense, everyone gets what they are looking for. The great non-Christian philosophers are in the first circle of hell. They do not have the ecstasy that comes with the dancing and laughing in heaven, but they got what they were looking for—a serene lack of activity. As one descends into hell, one finds that others got what they were looking for also. For example, those who were chasing after passion get passion in spades and are whipped around by a wind of passion. But now the passion is unmitigated by the grace of God and is no longer pleasant.

As the descent into hell continues, one finally comes to the center or core of hell. It is not hot, but cold, very cold. In the center of hell, Satan is frozen up to his waist in a lake. The lake is kept frozen by the flapping of his own wings. The reader understands that he is flapping his wings in anger. Satan is chewing on three traitors, and he is chewing what Dante later calls the "eternal empty grudge." One could even assume that the grudge is that the world is not the way that Satan believes it should be.

Here is the part that strikes me. As Dante and Virgil continue to descend and get out of hell, we realize that everything in hell is, in a way, upside down. Dante has to reverse the position of his feet as he begins to move toward God's country and the light. What he thought was right side up in hell turns out to be upside down as he sees the stars. He had been so long in that world of separation and twisted values that he thought he was right side up when he was in hell. He was wrong.

Here is the heart of the upside-down leader. In a time when the world is insane, an upside-down leader may really turn out to be right side up. It would be dangerous to be too concerned about the latest fashions in hell, or to strive to be consistent with them.

After a long time, when Dante finally gets to heaven, he sees angels dancing hand in hand in a circle. They are there on the first circle of heaven. Dante asks them if they want to move up to another circle. The angels look at him as if he is crazy. Such a question is really a hellish question. The angels reply that their joy comes from doing the will of God, wherever that may be.

This story is worth thinking about. If we try to get too "cutting edge" in this world, we may find ourselves simply striving to move up through some set of gradations. In doing so, we may get off-track and find ourselves serving the wrong kingdom. Somehow, along the way, we can slowly begin to think that moving up to the next circle is actually the point. But then, if the world sometimes is like a mental institution, we probably don't want to win the contests set by those who are deranged. Better to be quiet and purposeful. In fact, if we find ourselves immersed in the values of some infernal institution with all of its ethics, we might actually need to look down instead of up.

principle #7
Don't Just Do Something, Stand There

Don't underestimate the value of Doing Nothing, of just going along, listening to all the things you can't hear, and not bothering.

Piglet in *Pooh's Little Instruction Book*

Gentle Diligence

*I*n challenging times, a real leader will just naturally take charge. You can watch it with humans, and with dogs, and with other animals. However, every true leader must remember the importance of not taking charge.

I am not talking about being a slug. This principle is not an excuse for being lazy. Francis de Sales, the spiritual advisor, has a wonderful expression for describing the way that we should go about things. He says there are two kinds of diligence. One kind of diligence can bring great visible results in the short run, but can turn out to be destructive in unintended ways because this kind of diligence may surge into a situation like a bull in a china shop. Even if it doesn't affect others negatively, it can have deleterious consequences for the person engaged in the activity. De Sales calls this kind of diligence "violent diligence."

On the other hand, there is a kind of quiet persistence that is sometimes not noticed, but is able to bring long-term results that bless many people. De Sales calls this "quiet diligence." For me, quiet diligence means resisting the temptation to surge in and fix everything immediately. This kind of diligence may be able to hear God's instructions because it is not so frenetically active. I have learned in my own life that it is very hard to hear God when I am "violently" diligent.

In the East, there is a saying: muddy waters, when still, become clear. If there is a God, and the premise of this book is that there is, then being quiet may be the most important thing that a leader can do. Remember, the situation may be something more like algebra and in comparison, we may have the mental capabilities of a cat.

Addicting Themselves to Work

Brother Lawrence is an unleader to me, because he stayed in the shadows and seemed to be doing very little, except washing pots and pans. He was a simple lay brother in a Christian community in Paris over 300 years ago. Yet he had committed to stay in the love of God and practice the presence of God no matter what the task, be it large or small. He was attentive to doing for God the things we normally do for ourselves. He wrote no books, but people came to him to ask him about his attentiveness to God's presence. He seemed from the outside to be doing very little, to have held a low position in his order. Most people wouldn't know Brother Lawrence's superior's name, or his superior's superior's name, and on and on. However, we do know and are grateful for Brother Lawrence's way of staying in his quiet place, and responding to those who saw that he was practicing something in the kitchen that was available to all people, regardless of their place on any social ladder.

So often a leader feels as if he or she has to do something, to perhaps change something in the leader's use of time, as some leadership self-help books suggest. Brother Lawrence comes at things from a different angle. He suggests the exact opposite. We don't have to do or change anything. I think that this is a huge insight in the journey of the unbeliever. This is the way Brother Lawrence puts it in one of his conversations:

> That our sanctification did not depend upon changing our works, but in doing that for God's sake which we commonly do for our own. That it was lamentable to see how many people mistook

the means for the end, addicting themselves to certain works, which they performed very imperfectly, by reason of their human or selfish regards.

There we go, mistaking ends for means, working hard to change the environment, becoming literally addicted to activities. Notice that Brother Lawrence uses the language of an addiction in describing people who want to add more works in order to attain sanctification. Instead, Brother Lawrence suggests that we *do* nothing different, but only that we stop, and do for God the things we normally do for ourselves. Astonishing.

Get Out of the Way

I love to look at the last instructions Jesus gave to the disciples in Acts before He ascends to heaven. He doesn't tell them to witness or go change society or even preach the good news in Acts. He tells them to wait. "He ordered them not to depart from Jerusalem, but to wait for the promise of the Father" (Acts 1:4). In a sense, after they wait and receive the Holy Spirit, they will naturally be witnesses.

Sometimes God may instruct us to do an activity, and we may need to do it quickly and in a timely fashion. But sometimes God tells us to do nothing. When the people of God are trapped between a body of water and the most advanced army of the ancient world, I imagine the Hebrew leadership-type people are scanning the crowd looking for some leader who will do something. Yet God gives Moses this instruction: "The Lord will fight for you, and you have only to be silent" (Exodus 14:14).

This instruction conveys a deep truth to me. So often we assume that how we respond is of primary importance. Well, it is important. In the Bible, our actions have important consequences. We're not just zero. What we do makes a difference. But on another level, God has many ways to do things. It is His activity that is working. If we take our part too seriously, we miss the point. Then sometimes we try to play a role that was never assigned to us.

I heard someone quote Meister Eckhardt, an ancient Christian mystic, as saying all God wants is for us to get out of the way. This approach to leadership can free us up.

My friend and I laugh about a time years ago when he was deeply troubled and was seeking if there were something more than just existing. We talked for hours about God and Jesus. As the conversation got more intense, I needed to go to the bathroom. When I returned, I asked him an important question. "Do you want to ask Christ into your life right now?"

He said, "I just did, when you were in the bathroom." All God needed was to get me out of the way. Even a bathroom break can be a divine appointment.

Of course, there is a power in doing. But the leader needs to remember that sometimes there is a power in not doing. Some people joke about what General Custer said when he finally had in sight the village with thousands of Lakota and Cheyenne warriors. He ended up surrounded with only 200 cavalry. As he saw their operations at first, he is said to have exclaimed, "Hurrah, boys, now we have them!" and then led the charge to his own annihilation. Not a great military move.

The Power of Thunderous Silence

Some leaders have forgotten the power of not doing. Having labored in New York City for a long time, I remember working with an organization that helps religious groups in poor neighborhoods begin to work together to change their neighborhoods for good. They were community organizers.

I will never forget one of the meetings with the elected officials of our area. The premise of the meetings was that these officials were people elected to serve the needs of our community. Instead of being allowed to talk on and on about whatever they wanted to, each politician was given two minutes. We had a timekeeper. Each politician was asked if he or she would support the issue we were working on. If they did not answer the question, or if they began to veer into some automatic response that they had said a hundred times before, the facilitator had a right to interrupt the speaker and get them back on track. They were asked to say yes or no to supporting a particular issue.

If the speaker said yes, they would support the specific action we were supporting, thunderous and good-natured applause came from the 500 people we promised beforehand would be there. But if the speaker said no, they would not support the specific action, we had been trained to be totally silent. No boos, no movement, just thunderous silence. This silence was one of the most powerful things I had ever experienced in a community meeting. The silence so disconcerted one politician, that after he said no, he continued to perspire and equivocate on the platform as he saw the silent faces. Within the time period of about a minute, he had talked himself around to saying yes. Again the thunderous and good-natured applause. But the yes would not have happened without a crowd who had been specifically trained to do nothing at the appropriate time.

One of the greatest things our culture has forgotten is the value of silence. David in the Psalms understood this value. In order to live, he had to keep his mouth shut in the land of Gath and act as though he were mentally ill, making marks on the door of the gate (1 Samuel 21:13). We know that not speaking was important to David, because we hear it in the lyrics of his songs. "I said I will guard my ways, that I may not sin with my tongue; I will guard my mouth with a muzzle, so long as the wicked are in my presence" (Psalm 39:1). As a leader for many people, he saw the value of guarding his words. "Set a guard, O Lord, over my mouth; keep watch over the door of my lips!" (Psalm 141:3).

The Power of Not Networking

A leader needs prudence as well as aggressiveness. Centuries ago Mencius in China made this comment: "Let people decide firmly what they will not do, and they will be free to do vigorously what they ought to do." Too often there is shrapnel from the leaders who only know the things that they will do, and not the things that they will not do. Not every situation requires the leader to come out with his guns blazing. Some circumstances require open ears instead of opening fire.

Clearly God uses times that seem unproductive to us in powerful ways. One can see how God used the times when someone was forgotten. Joseph was forgotten in jail. Moses spent his 40 years in the desert. Paul spent three years in Arabia. Changes are going on in these persons during these times, which we could probably not articulate, even if we did understand them.

Some leadership books talk about always networking, never eating alone, learning the art of reaching out and making the first impression, building your web of relationships into a powerful force. In light of the experience of these biblical characters, perhaps sometimes it is important not to network, to eat alone, not to fill your life with endless contacts. It may be well sometime to refuse to be active. Like Jeremiah, perhaps sometimes we are to sit alone, so that we can eventually "utter what is precious, and not what is worthless" (Jeremiah 15: 19).

Leading Groups by Shutting Up

*D*oing nothing can bring out others in a powerful way. When we started our church, a man who was formerly homeless attended. One day he told me he thought he was called to teach. At the time, we had no Bible Study with our worship service, so I asked him to teach a class for the adults.

I remember sitting in with him on the first session. The session should have been an hour. The man was totally finished with his material in ten minutes. I cringed and fidgeted in my seat, acutely aware that I could have done much better, filling the room with my educated intelligence. One thing about this man made me particularly uncomfortable. He would ask a question, and if no one answered, he would just wait. And wait. And wait. It was excruciating to me, that much awkward silence, that much doing nothing in a group. I writhed in my seat in silent agony. The uncomfortable quiet was a visible sign that our group was a failure. I longed to intervene.

Yet as time progressed, I noticed an amazing thing. Some people, who never talked at any of our other activities, began to speak after the long, long silences. They participated in this group, although they didn't participate in any of the groups led by much more able leaders. I think that they participated in this quiet group for a reason. In the other groups, they were overwhelmed by the leaders, who must have seemed like "super Christians" who kept a non-stop, vibrantly interesting discussion going on. On the other hand, that formerly homeless man, with his ability to do nothing and remain silent, turned out to the best teacher of all for those people beaten down by their own inabilities.

Sometimes people need someone to do nothing in the middle of emergencies. Once a counselor was teaching our staff how to handle people in a crisis. He said something I will never forget. A lot of times, people in the middle of a crisis situation don't need you to do anything. What they need most of all is one person who is the quiet in the midst of a storm. Leaders with a lot of experience with crisis know that often what they are is quiet in the midst of the storm. They don't have to do anything.

The Right Word at the Right Time

It is important sometimes to do nothing so that we can hear. Dietrich Bonhoeffer one time said that in order to speak the words of God, we must listen with the ears of God. No wonder some Christians cultivate the discipline of a quiet time. "Morning by morning he awakens, he awakens my ear," Isaiah says (50:4). By allowing our ears to awaken, we are able to sustain with a word the one who is weary.

According to God in Isaiah, God awakens our ears so that we can actually sustain a person with a word. If I have learned anything in helping promote programs that tutor children and at-risk youth, I have learned that words are very powerful. As Proverbs 18:21 says, life and death are in the power of what we say. If part of blessing means to empower to succeed, and part of cursing means to empower to fail, we can bless or curse a child easily with words. Just tell a child you know they can't do it each day and you will eventually empower the child to fail. Just tell a child each day that you knew they could do it, and you help empower the child to succeed.

A trainer came to our ministry to train our tutors for a day. As the day progressed, he told a little bit of his story. He had grown up on the Lower East Side, and he had had a pretty rough life with a chaotic family structure. He said that when he was 12 years old, a gymnastics teacher came to their tutoring program to teach about gymnastics. The teacher was fun and full of life and all the kids loved him. During the time the gymnastics teacher was there, he watched this little 12-year old persistently do his turns in front of him, and the teacher said four words—"This kid won't quit."

In looking back at himself as a 12-year old, the adult trainer told us, "If those words weren't true before he said them, they were true after he said them. I went on to middle school and I would say to myself 'I'm a kid that doesn't quit.' I went on to high school and on to college. Whenever I had a rough time, I would say, 'I am someone who doesn't quit.'" I sat in the training and saw how that adult trainer was blessing so many, and I thought about those four words. They were four simple words that had such an effect on him and through him such an effect on so many other tutors and kids he had consequently helped. I also thought about that gymnastic teacher 20 years ago who had said those words. Did he realize at the end of that day what he had done for that little boy? I doubt it. But I am so glad he said those four words.

Each of us can probably remember thoughtless words from others that tended to curse us, and powerful words from others that encouraged us to succeed. Words are some of the most important things we have in life. If we don't stop to listen with the ears of God, to let God waken our ears, it is very hard for us to speak those words, soaked in God's Spirit, that really bless a bent reed or a flickering lamp. A leader who is always busy, rushed and impatient by the importance of what is being done, is often not able to speak the true word of power because he has rarely stopped doing things long enough to listen with the ears of God.

The Commandment We Forgot

*E*very person has a chance to practice doing nothing each week. It is one of the "big ten," as in Ten Commandments, and many leaders totally ignore it. It is the only commandment that talks about remembering, as if we have somehow forgotten, as if we have let something very important drift away. It is the commandment to remember the Sabbath (Exodus 20:8), or remember the day of rest. This is our chance to practice doing nothing and letting God work out His plan in some deep subterranean way that we are not even equipped to fathom. It is our recognition that it is important sometimes to just stand there. It is a weekly lesson that not doing anything may help more get done.

I am amazed at how many Christian leaders do not follow this practice, and it is something you have to practice. These leaders are too busy, their work is too important, they have too much to do, though they smile thoughtfully, knowing that really the counsel to rest is right. I know that some people think keeping the day of rest is a legalistic practice, but in reality it is so wonderful that no one ought to miss it.

On the day of rest, you look back over all you have done in the week, just as God looked back over His work, and you say the things that are good. You refuse to do all the productive things that the world or your job tells you must be done. You let go of the emails, the texts, the appointments, and papers. You rest. You reflect on God's goodness. You put all the things that must be done aside. It is delicious. You recite God's Word—"It is vain for you to rise up early and go late to rest, eating the bread of anxious toil; for he gives to his beloved sleep" (Psalm 127:2).

Does God need to rest? I don't know. I do know that when my sons were small, and I wanted them to take a nap, I would lie down on the bed and take a nap with them. What if God simply wanted you to take a nap? Refusing to take a rest exposes the heart of the worldly system of leadership. The supposed leader becomes so important to everything that he cannot take even 24 hours of rest once during the week. He is simply too important to all the work. He has set some plans and he is determined to fulfill them regardless.

Unleaders recognize that they will never have enough time to do even the things they think that they ought to do. Of course, they never have enough time to do all the things that other people think they ought to do. However, they have exactly enough time to do what God wants them to do. That's why God can say in Isaiah, "Whoever believes will not be in haste" (Isaiah 28:16). A day of rest each week reminds me that I am not to lead, but to follow. My Master is gentle and kind, and He says come to Him and He will give me rest. His yoke is really easy (Matthew 11:28–30). Where did I get that other idea, about how hard it is to follow Christ? From the world's view of leadership. Before you know it, you are caught up in the world's system of leadership and you are indispensible, a sad little idol to yourself caught up in a system that is dead wrong. Christian work can take up the same scam. Your work is so important. No one can do these things but you. You are pouring yourself out in endless days and sleepless nights for the Lord. I will say it again. I think that script is a scam. You can identify these leaders because they are always talking about how hard the Christian life is. They have forgotten that Jesus says His yoke is easy.

Here are the two practical suggestions I give to young people who are working in ministry. The pressure to do it all is so great. First, if someone asks you to do something on your designated Sabbath day, two words can save your life. The caller will always work to tell you that the breakfast meeting, the phone conference, the visit is essential to your work. It can't be missed. And the more times you accept their pitch, the more things will take up that one day of the week you had so feebly and with such good intentions set aside. These are the two words—"previous commitment." You say, "Oh, I am so sorry; I cannot do that early morning meeting that is so important. I have a previous commitment." I have used those words hundreds of times and no one has ever asked me what my previous commitment was. Your previous commitment might be to sit with your pajamas on and drink coffee and watch cartoons with your little kids. That's your business.

The other practical suggestion I have is never to say yes to a request for a commitment immediately. Just make it a rule. Otherwise, our idolatrous desire to please will rise up and say yes in the heat of the moment in spite of ourselves. Just say, "Thanks so much for thinking of me—let me check my calendar and get back to you tomorrow." You have just given yourself time to consider the commitment in prayer. Also, if you are like me, it is hard to say no to something that is well-intentioned and noble. If I get a sense in prayer that the request is not a task that I am to do, then I have time to rehearse and practice the way I will say no. Sounds silly, but it has helped me many times. We sometimes say in our ministry here in New York City, "In order to say the holy yes, you must say the holy no." Without some discerning rest, we tend to say yes to everything, and we can simply start going through the motions of work, and it will begin to feel as if we have the spiritual flu. At worst, if we don't say no to activities, we can implode.

Without a chance to simply stand there and do nothing, we will eventually become resentful of the people God has called us to help, as well as irritated at our co-workers. I have seen it happen so many times. A person is secretly furious at the people around them, because that angry person is working so much harder than anyone else around. If you ask that person when was the last time he or she took a day off, it has usually been a long, long time. It is amazing how many times this is true. It is almost like an equation. It has happened to me. I know that when I am getting angry and irritated at the people around me, it is often a red light on the dashboard indicating that I need to be obedient in resting. My wife, Susan, has her own way of reminding me of this, as I rush off to that critically important meeting that eats into the one day we have carved out to rest in the Lord. She says, "You know, they stoned people to death in the Old Testament when they didn't take a day off."

Without taking a day of rest, it is very hard to see God's loving activities through the urgent circumstances that daily seem to slap us in the face. Everything seems like a mountain when we are exhausted. It is amazing how, after a good night's sleep and a bit of rest, the same circumstances that were mountains the day before seem like molehills. That's why God put this commandment in the "big ten."

It seems as though the leaders of our time, including Christian leaders, have forgotten this simple rule. They have forgotten how important it is sometimes to merely stop doing anything and stand there. The simple truth is that we have become overwired to take action in every single situation, regardless of what it is. We do this at our own hazard.

It really is hard for me to believe that sometimes it is most important simply to stand there. As a boy, I was so upset that Jesus didn't just send those twelve legions of angels down to wipe out the bad guys when He was arrested. That's the way to correct the problem. Just do it. Instead, Jesus did nothing. Then when He was on trial, it seemed to me to be the time to argue most passionately and eloquently for God's way. Instead, Jesus just stood there and answered nothing. I wonder if some people at the time interpreted His lack of activity as weakness, fear, or incompetence. He seems the exact opposite of what a forceful leader should do. Almost upside down.

principle #8
Think Inside the Box

What if "outside the box" was inside a bigger box?

Martin R. on the internet somewhere . . .

The Walls of a Playground

*M*y wife loves an old cartoon that shows a box with kitty litter and it says something like this: "It is good to think outside the box, unless you're a cat." Of course, it is good and often helpful to be creative. The danger comes, however, when creativity itself becomes the goal.

The culture of talking about thinking outside of the box has gotten out of hand. Everyone now is trying so hard to be outside the box, that if you are inside the box, you're really outside.

A box represents confinement, and no one at present wants to be confined. To be in a box means to have walls or boundaries around you. Isn't the goal of life to transcend those boundaries, to get beyond the walls?

Well, yes and no. There is just something in us that does not like a wall. In one way, the whole call of Christ is to free us from those walls. But in another way, we choose limitations. We choose the narrow way. In fact, there is something in us that needs a wall.

G. K. Chesterton has a provocative saying. It is true that doctrines and disciplines of faith have walls, he indicates, "but they are the walls of a playground." He paints the picture of children playing next to a cliff. If the walls and protection are knocked down, the child is huddled and afraid, never quite knowing when an overactive game might send her over the edge. In fact, the child is not quite sure where the edge is.

Restrictions are not always bad. I remember traveling to the mile-high bridge in North Carolina. Beforehand, I was very solicitous of my wife who doesn't really love heights. I, on the other hand, had worked as a roofer in college, and I looked forward to getting on the bridge. Yet when we actually got to the bridge, it became clearer to me how it worked. You walk out in single file on the bouncing bridge and hold tightly to the railing on both sides. Sure enough, it was Susan who lingered and walked slowly, enjoying the view, stopping to lean over the side railings to look down. On the other hand, I was hanging on pretty tightly, just as ready to move on as to linger. Susan had found that the railings helped her to enjoy something that we couldn't have enjoyed otherwise. Afterward, I looked back and tried to imagine how fearful the walk would have been if we had simply the single-file bridge and no railings. It would have been terrifying. I could never see those particular railings as confining. We couldn't have gone across the bridge without them.

From Great to Good

*I*n one way or other, leaders always have to deal with an "ethical box" as they deal with the challenges of life. Leaders voluntarily put great restraints on themselves in some ways if they say that the ends do not justify the means. To say that ends do not justify the means puts ethics over results. But we have already said, forget results. To treat people decently, to refuse to lie, to refuse to cut corners in the midst of an important project is certainly a lot easier to talk about than to do. At least it is for me.

One of the great leadership books of the last decade was the book *From Good to Great*. Perhaps we need a companion book that is titled *From Great to Good*. Perhaps we need to stop thinking about being a great leader in terms of results. Perhaps we need to stop talking about being great altogether for a while. What if being good ethically did not lead to being great in terms of the results for the company?

I wonder if great leaders don't know intuitively that they live inside a box, an ethical box, a narrow box that limits many options they might take as they lead. A leader needs to be reminded of all the things that cannot be done in this twisting and turning life.

I remember as a teenager reading a book by Mohandas K. Gandhi called *Experiment with Truth*. In this book, as I remember, Gandhi described his early days of being a lawyer. He refused to lie, and he refused to defend a person he felt was guilty. This approach tended to limit the number of clients he had and was an obvious problem for business. The results of his choices were not at first impressive.

Yet the results of assuming an ethical "box" can go in all different directions. Eventually Gandhi had a booming business. One reason was that he was a good and competent lawyer. Another reason was that only people who thought they had a good and true case went to him. Once ethics trumps results, you never know what might happen. This approach to a career made quite an impression on me as a high schooler.

Inside a Soap Box

So far I have been talking about thinking inside the box in terms of the importance of maintaining one's ethics and one's integrity regardless of results. But sometimes remembering what is inside the box really helps you find the most productive answer even on a physical level.

I remember reading about a Japanese company that made soaps. They had a problem. Sometimes the assembly line would allow a box of soap to get by that did not contain any soap. The managers could not think of an efficient way to solve the problem. They hired some consultants who attacked the problem with vigor. They were efficiency experts. After much analysis and study, they designed an x-ray machine along the assembly line that would show a worker whenever a box went by that did not have soap in it. The new machine was enormously expensive, costing tens of thousands of dollars, but it accomplished the desired results. But with all their expertise, they had forgotten what was inside the problem soap boxes. Nothing. As the x-ray machine was being installed, a manager noticed that an assembly line worker had already solved the problem. He had simply put an inexpensive house fan next to the assembly line. Every time an empty box went by, the fan blew it off the line. Problem solved. The assembly line worker had simply remembered how light the inside of a soap box actually was.

Maybe this is the way to put it. Placing so much attention on thinking outside the box can become a box or a confinement itself. Maybe the answer doesn't lie outside the box. As in the solution found by the factory worker, maybe remembering the inside of the box, even what is *not* in the inside of the box, like a heavy piece of soap, can help you find the answer. Checking the old or simple way may be the path to the new.

The Narrow Way Is a Broad Way

*M*any things can be portrayed as a confinement or a box. Marriage is commonly portrayed in movies as a box, a confinement to break out of. And yet, sometimes, when one truly commits to that box and limits oneself in a thousand ways for the sake of the spouse, something wonderful can happen—a new kind of trust and liberty in life. Committing your time and loyalty to one friend can feel like a box, but when you are with that one friend, a freedom can come that you would never have with mere acquaintances. Children can seem like a total ball and chain on your life, but no one can really describe that experience of pouring yourself out for a little child, and the expansion of the heart that comes from it.

It is so strange—Jesus doesn't talk positively about a wonderful, broad, expansive way. He talks about a narrow way. A long time ago, my wife and I taught at a college in Hong Kong. When we were there, we visited an establishment started by former Buddhist monks who had become Christians. The symbol they used was a small cross (the truths of Christ) coming out of a large lotus flower (Buddhism). They felt as though Christ were the fulfillment of many things they were searching for. They had a wall around their monastery, and as we walked, I saw a tiny, and I mean tiny, door with some Chinese above it. I asked the person I was with what the Chinese said. He translated it into English: Enter into the narrow way. I sucked in my breath and crouched down, and with much effort, finally got through the door. On the other side was a surprise—a panoramic view of the entire countryside. Without confining myself through that little doorway, I would have never seen the mountains, the trees, the sky. I was entranced, and I have never forgotten the experience. Sometimes taking on the confinement of a box can bring a freedom we never dreamed of.

principle #9
Become a Nobody

I'm Nobody! Who are you?
Are you – Nobody – too?

Author Emily Dickinson

You Can't Give What You Don't Have

A long time ago I worked in a community service in San Francisco with some Franciscan brothers and sisters. I was struggling with what I would do next. I wasn't fulfilling the expectations of some of the people in my family. I felt I didn't have a clue. I saw a poster, kind of a recruiting poster, with a picture of Francis of Assisi, with his silly shaved spot on his head with his funny clothes and his rope for a belt. The words underneath the poster simply said this—"Become a Nobody." The words struck me because, at the time, everyone seemed to be telling everyone else that they must affirm that they are *somebody*.

You can't give up what you don't have. Some people need to say to themselves. "I am somebody." The upside-down part of Jesus' message is that once you know who you are, you can give it up. The first step is to know who we are. We are royalty and the Bible says we will reign with Christ. We are a "chosen race, a royal priesthood, a holy nation, a people for his own possession" (1 Peter 2:9). David says God gives us steadfast love and mercy like a crown (Psalm 103:4). Wow. Sometimes I ask this question in a group of people, many of whom are homeless—When David, who was already anointed as king, had to act like he was crazy and had no place to stay, was he then any less of a king? The answer I usually get is a "no." When Jesus had no place to lay His head, was He any less than king then? Not really. The point is that circumstances in the end don't really affect this astonishing, royal value that God gives to us.

An amazing thing can happen. Once that really soaks in and moves from the head to the heart, you can sit at the lowest place at the table. You can be last. The wandering homeless King who was crucified has showed us the way. Once you really know who you are, you can bend down and wash someone's stinking feet. You can work and not be recognized or thanked.

I know that it's easy to talk about, very easy. It's even easier to talk about when you have a lot of cultural and social advantages. Still, I don't know about you, but I want people to see the good things I do and think well of me. But this striving to be somebody can become its own little god. A universe of striving people can become its own dead end. However, the urge to be recognized is so strong.

Here is the way I explain it in New York City. Derek Jeter is currently a baseball icon for many New Yorkers. If Derek Jeter came to our park on the Lower East Side and played baseball with our kids at Graffiti Church, he wouldn't be fighting and shoving to be the first one at bat. He wouldn't be desperate to get to the front of the line to show everyone how good a batter he is. Of course not. He would let every child go first. He wouldn't even have to bat at all. He knows who he is. He knows how well he can bat. He doesn't have to prove it to anybody. Likewise, when we truly know who we are in Christ, we can stay in the background. We can become a nobody. It doesn't matter. Regardless of how hard or how strange the circumstances are now, we know that there will be a time when God will wipe away every tear from our eyes (Revelation 21:4).

/// leadership /// upside down /// leadership ///
upside down /// leadership /// upside down /// upside
/// leadership /// upside down /// leadership

When You Don't Care
Who Gets the Credit

I saw a leader who knew who she was as she was working for the homeless in New York City. She never looked for recognition, and often she didn't get it. But when she began to work for others, things began to happen. Organizations were formed. Funds came in. Interpersonal relationships were solved. People's lives were changed and we didn't even see how. But if you looked closely, you could see her gentle direction behind the scenes, doing the tedious work no one wanted to do in order to make the dreams happen, letting someone else get the credit. I thought of what Harry Truman once said: "It is amazing what you can accomplish if you do not care who gets the credit."

When we begin to look at the world in this way, some leaders who seem to demand a great deal of attention from others seem less important. We begin to see these other kinds of leaders, these wonderful invisible unleaders, who move through the stream of life, blessing others, doing the unnoticed thing, not needing recognition. Once we understand this, our world takes on a new drama. Heroes surround us, doing the small insignificant things that move the world, gladiators for good in the struggles concerning the most trivial activities, soaked in the quiet love of God. Once we see these, some of the other, more vociferous and articulate leaders sound like bullfrogs. How could we have been so blind?

The preacher in Ecclesiastes has a wonderful story about a poor man who saved the city, but no one really notices or remembers. The preacher sees it as an example of wisdom:

"I have also seen this example of wisdom under the sun, and it seemed great to me. There was a little city with few men in it, and a great king came against it and besieged it, building great siegeworks against it. But there was found in it a poor, wise man, and he by his wisdom delivered the city. Yet no one remembered that poor man. But I say that wisdom is better than might, though the poor man's wisdom is despised and his words are not heard" (Ecclesiastes 9:13-16).

If the preacher is identified as Solomon, then we have one of the wisest and greatest leaders in the Bible speaking. He notices this poor, wise man who saves a city and no one remembers. Still, Solomon sees this poor man's wisdom as better than the might of the great king with all his soldiers and his siegeworks. He makes this statement about the poor man, even though the poor man's wisdom is looked down upon and his words are not actually heard. What an unusual thing for a great king like Solomon to say.

This book began with a picture of an upside-down man, Adoniram Judson. But his story would not have been told without his remarkably resourceful first wife and companion, Ann Judson. While he was hanging upside down, literally immobilized, she was negotiating with officials, cajoling guards, answering questions from interrogators, avoiding arrest herself, and praying always. Her refusal to despair, her grit in the face of mockery, and her remarkable social intelligence saved her husband's life again and again. And she wrote about it. Her faithful heart for her husband, in the midst of the degradation and disease she eventually endured, and her refusal to be in the center of attention, makes her a true unleader. I wouldn't be writing about the upside down leader, if it weren't for her.

Other cultures have understood this quiet power sometimes better than we have. In the East, I remember hearing a number of stories about a person who arrives in a group and somehow things begin to go right. Nerves are calmed. People begin to work together. Goals are achieved. Yet no one notices how this person is assisting. Somehow, in some non-conceptual way, just the person's being there helps things begin to come into balance. Once I heard these stories, I began to remember situations in my own life where someone's quiet presence seemed to help everyone work together. These people rarely got recognition for it.

A novelist in the twentieth century tried to catch this sense that Christianity has almost lost. In *The Journey to the East*, by Hermann Hesse, the protagonist goes on a journey as part of a League. He does not even realize who the President of the League is until much later after he has lost his way for a long time. It turns out to be the servant, the friendly porter on the journey who has done all the menial tasks for the other, more important members of the trip. He had done all the work in such a natural and unaffected way that he was hardly noticed. Robert Greenleaf found this story very provocative and used it as he developed a new way to lead in the corporate world called "Servant Leadership." It sounded so new when it first came out, but he went back to the words of Jesus: "whoever would be first among you must be your slave" (Matthew 20:27).

Heroes in the Little Things

I don't mind washing someone's feet on Maundy Thursday, or some other special Christian ceremony, especially if other people see me do it. Still, I'm not all that happy about cleaning the toilets at church. As one of our teachers at church sometimes says, "If cleaning the bathroom doesn't seem very important to you, wait until you are there and don't have any toilet paper."

It is hard for us to evaluate the small things. The person who quietly tutors children through the years does not get the recognition of someone who physically stops a gang member from hurting a child. Those people who violently stop a gang member from hurting someone else may get their name in the paper. They may be called heroes. But we could never quantify the children who did not become gang members because of that quiet tutor. In working in the aftermath of 9/11 in Lower Manhattan, I adapted a phrase from Abraham Joshua Heschel's *I Asked for Wonder*. Heschel wrote, "We have failed to fight *for* right, *for* justice, *for* goodness; as a result we must fight *against* wrong, *against* injustice, *against* evil." In shortened form, he said that if we don't fight for what is right, we end up *only* fighting against what is wrong.

We in our work in the Lower East Side made a commitment to do the little unseen things to help in our neighborhood to fight for what is right, so that noticeable heroes don't have to fight so hard against what is wrong. People who fight for what is right often don't get the same recognition as those who end up fighting against what is wrong. However, once we understand who we really are, that lack of recognition is really not a problem.

/// The Old Boy

Somewhere around 2,500 years ago, a man lived who was given the name that translates to "the Old Boy" or "the Old Fellow " or perhaps "the Grand Old Master" (Lao Tzu). He was a unique man, and it is said that even Confucius came to visit him once and found him baffling.

"It is good to think outside the box, unless you're a cat."At the end of his life, the story goes that the Old Fellow sought more solitude and got on a water buffalo and headed west to what is now Tibet. It is said that a gatekeeper begged him to leave some written record of his beliefs for civilization. The Old Fellow agreed and returned with a thin volume called "The Way and Its Power. " You can read it in a half-hour, and some of it to me sounds like the Sermon on the Mount. The Old Fellow had some things to say about a leader:

> *"A leader is best*
> > *When people barely know that he exists.*
> *. . . Of a good leader, who talks little,*
> > *When his work is done, his aim fulfilled, they will all say,*
> *"We did this ourselves."*

This is a style of leadership that becomes more apparent when people tire of the slick boosterism and braggadocio of some leaders. Maybe I should say this quiet kind of leader becomes less and less apparent as more and more is done.

When No One Notices You

Oswald Chambers wrote a lot about how this kind of service works. He said that you really know that God is working when no one notices you at all:

> "If you are rightly devoted to the Lord Jesus, you have reached the sublime height where no one ever thinks of noticing you, all that is noticed is that the power of God comes through you all the time."

There is a wonderful old urban short story called "Passing of the Third Floor Back" by Jerome K. Jerome. In this story a stranger comes to a dingy boarding house in a dingy neighborhood in the city. The environment among the boarders is petty and mean-spirited. The stranger doesn't do anything dramatic or forceful. He simply lives there and talks to the landlady and the boarders. In each person he talks to, he assumes a goodness that goes beyond the cynicism and mean-spirited self-concern that each one presents. Soon the entire building changes, and takes on a decency and goodness that no worldly-wise person would have anticipated. The stranger really didn't do anything except go about his daily life. Despite all our discussions of city directives and government policies and urban activism in neighborhoods, this story makes one wonder what kind of leadership is most important. Eventually, the stranger quietly leaves with no fanfare.

When I was a missionary teaching at a college in Hong Kong, I came across a biography of Hudson Taylor. Hudson Taylor had helped start the China Inland Mission, which eventually assisted hundreds of missionaries, and he had insisted that they never ask for money. Hudson Taylor's personal qualities were not totally impressive to me. I remember putting down the book with the oddest feeling that I hadn't felt reading any other biography. I didn't finish the book thinking about what a great man Hudson Taylor was. Instead, I thought about what a great God our God is. I recently read about a time that Taylor was traveling on a train with his friend who was attempting to hide a very negative newspaper article about Taylor. The article said that the writer was expecting some great missionary, but was very disappointed in seeing Taylor. Hudson Taylor did not have an imposing personality or a great oratorical voice, and he elicited little applause. Taylor read the article and smiled. He said, "This is very just criticism, for it is all true. I have often thought that God made me little in order that He might show what a great God He is." Perhaps, sometimes, having a non-imposing persona could keep that person from being a block to the One who is far more important.

Foam on the Waves

Albert Schweitzer, the medical missionary left two promising careers to serve in Central Africa, received a lot of attention for his work and, eventually in 1952, received the Nobel Peace Prize. Although he influenced many lives, he wrote these words in his autobiography:

> "Of all the will toward the ideal in mankind only a small part can manifest itself in public action. All the rest of this force must be content with small and obscure deeds. The sum of these, however, is a thousand times stronger than the acts of those who receive wide public recognition. The latter, compared to the former, are like the foam on the waves of a deep ocean"
>
> — *Out of My Life and Thought*

What a startling way to see the work of those who are publicly recognized. Most of our books of history focus on the key personalities that shaped an era. Perhaps it is just the way our minds are made. We can't see anything else. But Schweitzer helps us think of all those thousands of unseen acts as the true ocean, and the leaders who get most of the acclaim are simply the foam on the waves.

At the end of the Sermon on the Mount (Matthew 7:21–23) Jesus makes a strange comment on those who are not really obeying but get a lot of attention in life saying religious words and working wonderful religious miracles. Surely, this kind of activity is what we want, isn't it — people shouting out, "Lord, Lord," and doing all kinds of miracles in Jesus' name? Jesus' comment about them is telling and decisive. He says to them, "Depart from me. I never knew you."

principle #10
Embrace Shame

No great man thinks he is great, and no small man thinks he is small.

(often quoted by my father—source unknown)

When You Are on the Ropes

Jesus is so counterintuitive. It goes against my grain. Even though we have had 2,000 years of verbiage commenting on His words about taking the lowest place at a gathering, everything in my peanut-sized soul squeaks out to get the top places. I will do it by clever social jockeying, by whatever means necessary, even if it means pretending to seek the lowest place so that I can be thought humble. I know, I know that what He says ought to be sincerely what we should do, but many people who stand out in the crowd don't take His track. Jesus seems to be heading us all in the wrong direction.

In the letter of 2 Corinthians, Paul looks as though he is on the ropes. Other superspiritual leaders have come to the church and spoken against him. He tells them that he has a sentence of death, but that it has all happened so that we can trust God, who raises people from the dead.

We talked earlier about the strange way that Paul asserts his leadership. I have never read anything quite like it. Paul gives his credentials, but eventually he brags about his weakness. He tells about being let down in a basket (11:33). As mentioned earlier, in the ancient world, the biggest hero receives "the crown of the wall" for being the first one to be at the top of the wall of a city. Contrary to what you would expect, Paul brags about being the one who gets to the bottom of the wall.

Responding to the superspiritual people who have diverted the group, he doesn't tell about some great time when God answered his prayer. On the contrary, he tells about a time that he prayed and his prayer was not answered. He says that he prayed it three times. No answer. Finally God said, "My grace is sufficient for you, for my power is made perfect in weakness" (12:9).

From the normal view, Paul's leadership responses just get stranger and stranger. "Therefore I will boast all the more gladly of my weaknesses, so that the power of Christ may rest upon me," he continues in the same verse.

There is a different model for leadership going on here. The direction for this approach comes from the Lord he serves. In the end, he refers to Christ. "For he was crucified in weakness, but lives by the power of God. For we also are weak in him, but in dealing with you we will live with him by the power of God" (13:4).

As one reads through the letter, the seemingly bizarre nature of Paul's approach begins to sink in. Weakness begins to become the envelope for God's power. Paul almost delights in weakness, seeing that weakness as evidence of the power of God. He isn't afraid to embrace what others, even in the Christian community, might think is shameful. How can that be?

Indecisive in New York

There are worse things than shame. Sometimes the avoidance of shame or embarrassment can keep us from doing what is right. Dietrich Bonhoeffer was a brilliant theologian and a natural leader who came from a well-known family committed to Germany. As Hitler's influence increased, Bonhoeffer saw that he would be drafted and he knew that he could not serve in the Nazi military, as much as he loved his country. He also knew that if he refused to serve, he would create tremendous problems for the group of churches he supported, churches that had broken away from the state church. He wrote a quick letter to Reinhold Niebuhr saying that an invitation from Union Seminary in New York City for Bonhoeffer to teach would resolve his dilemma. Niebuhr and a host of friends in America worked extremely hard to get Bonhoeffer the quick invitation he needed. Strings were pulled, many letters sent, bureaucratic hurdles were leapt over in order to help Bonhoeffer. He accepted the invitation and arrived in New York before there were more problems with the German authorities.

Bonhoeffer only stayed in New York City 26 days. It was the summer of 1939. He wandered the streets of Manhattan, unhappy, in doubt. He read in Isaiah that "he who believes does not flee." He eventually realized that he had to tell all the people whom he respected, the ones who had worked so hard for him, that he had made a mistake. He would have to go back to Germany right away, despite all the extraordinary measures that were taken by friends for him to come to America. He did so, painfully, through letters and lunches and contacts. It must have been hard for him to face those who had done so much for him and to seem so indecisive. Some of his friends felt he was acting foolishly to go back to Germany when it seemed to be reeling out of control. Bonhoeffer, however, felt a different kind of peace as he returned before the end of the summer.

By September of 1939 the war had begun. Bonhoeffer continued to have to make difficult choices with humiliating consequences as he lived inside Nazi Germany. He needed to do some kind of service, so those who were plotting against Hitler helped him become a Nazi agent in Military Intelligence. This cover helped him to continue to minister as a pastor and work to help overthrow the government. However, his position created great misunderstanding from some who looked up to him and felt his working with Military Intelligence was a clear betrayal of their convictions. Bonhoeffer continued to focus on what he felt God had called him to do regardless of the humiliations he felt, sometimes within his own confessing community. Interestingly enough, in the middle of unthinkable choices he was having to make each day to follow where he felt God was calling him. He was working on a long book. The book he was working on was a biblical and brilliant work on ethics. Eventually his part in a plot to destroy Hitler was exposed, and he was executed just weeks before the war was over. As two men in civilian clothes called him to leave the others, his fellow prisoners all knew by the words these men used that he was about to be hanged. After the quagmire of moral choices and misunderstandings, he turned to his friend. "This is the end," he said. "For me, the beginning."

My Gift of Absentmindedness

*T*wenty years ago I read a book about Francis of Assisi. I can't even find it anymore. But a sentence in the book struck me It said something like this: "People are not holy, not because they cannot overcome evil, but because they are unwilling to embrace shame."

Somehow this sentence touched my own fear of failure, my own fear of being humiliated. I was working with many people who lived in abandoned buildings, who seemed to be at the bottom of society. Yet some of them had transcendent, holy lives. They were unafraid of the shame that surrounded their circumstances. They lacked social skills, clothing, bathrooms, electricity, and often food, even as they worked in a society that had all these things. Yet some weren't afraid of the shame.

Their willingness to embrace shame was a great help to me in the beginnings of my living here. It helped me even in little ways, as I sought to learn how to be a minister in an environment that was so different. Desiring to be competent, I was painfully aware that I was a bit absent-minded. I was defensive about it and tried to cover it up.

Each week I went to do a worship service at a nursing home. At first, it felt like a zoo. A restroom door would fly open in the middle of the service and a bellow come forth demanding help. I didn't know whether to stop the sermon or keep preaching. Two people listening would get into a yelling match in the middle of the service (whispers were rare there). Many in wheelchairs stayed asleep during the entire service. The people there were not impressed with my rapier theological insight. They were not touched by my moving personal stories in the sermon. But they loved to see me forget something, a Bible, a hat, a coat. "You've forgotten your umbrella!" a manic woman would cackle. They would all roar with the joy of life flowing through them. I got to the point where when I left, I would say, "You know me, now did I forget anything?" They would beam and help me. It was the high point of the service. Now I've been converted. I am not ashamed any more. I bring my absentmindedness as my gift of ministry to this group; it is my best feature.

The Shortest Distance
Between Two Points

*I*f we are not careful, humiliating experiences can take on a weight in our life that is not really reflective of what is happening. Experiences that don't support our view of what we hope to do can be blown way out of proportion. I believe that part of becoming more mature in leadership is refusing to allow experiences of failure to become branding, paralyzing occurrences. We often speak of how God can draw a straight line with a crooked stick. But sometimes, as one radio preacher put it, the shortest distance between two points may be a zigzag. At least it *looks* like a huge zigzag from our point of view. So what?

I remember one of my most humiliating speaking experiences. I had prepared hard for the conference. I traveled a long way. But somehow, I found myself in a room with a group of young people who didn't know what I was doing there and clearly didn't care. I faltered and stumbled my way through the presentation. My face burned bright red as I realized how boring I sounded to them. I wanted to quit in the middle. The turnout was low, and my words were obviously meaningless. Afterward, I asked myself and God, "Why am I here? This was the most useless use of my time ever. I am just not cut out for this sort of thing." I was engulfed by a sense of failure, way out of proportion to the real event.

A year later a woman came and worked with our at-risk youth. She did a marvelous job. She raised her own support. She blessed countless teenagers in our neighborhood. Sometime later, she reminded me that she had first heard about our ministry at Graffiti through that very conference talk, the one that I felt was so completely useless. She was one of the few participants.

The whole speaking experience felt like such a zigzag to me, but God was drawing His own lines. At other times when I feel that I have utterly failed in speaking, I hold this little story to my heart. We never know what God might be doing and how.

There is no guarantee that God will show us every time He is doing something. In the Book of Job, the character Job never knows about the conversation between Satan the accuser and God. The reader sees it, but Job just has the mind-blowing experience of encountering God in the whirlwind, with all of God's almost endless questions. Even in the end, Job never sees the whole story.

Learning to Just Go with It

The Crucifixion was not just designed only to inflict pain. It was also designed to engender shame. Jesus was made to walk through the streets of Jerusalem, carrying the instrument of His execution. From what we can ascertain, He might have had to carry a sign, which was nailed above Him as He was killed. "Head Jew" might be a better way to catch the mocking racial nature of the taunt.

In the end, this route with Christ is not really about being a leader. It is about being a person. How does one deal with shame? Shame can be a prime motivator for what we do and for what we avoid doing.

One of my sisters is very tall. She never lets it bother her, even when people infer that it might be better if she were smaller and more petite. "Gee, you sure are tall," people will sometimes say at a party. My sister never hesitates to answer, "Yes, and I've decided to go with it," she says with a flair. "What can you do?" she says to me. "I'm not going to shrink in shame. There's nothing I can do about it." She makes it her best feature.

Humility has a wonderful side benefit. It leads to humor. Anything that will help us not take ourselves so seriously is good. In one of our Bible groups, we have a gospel comedian. First Corinthians tells us that in the New Testament Church, everyone could bring their gift to the worship. We decided that the one with the gift of comedy should bring a one-liner every week. If we can laugh before we read from the Word of God, it helps us not to take all our problems so seriously. Example: "I've got the body of a god," he says, and pats his belly, "Buddha."

When a new work team comes in to help in one of our programs, one of my favorite unleaders at Graffiti is introduced by his first name. He looks at the eager young workers with a curdling scowl. "That's my name in most states," he snarls. It takes the fresh newcomers to New York City a moment before they realize he is kidding.

In Proverbs 3:7, the Bible tells us three things to do in order to receive healing to our flesh. The first one is "be not wise in your own eyes." Humor is a great discipline to keep us from being way too stuffy, too wise in our own eyes. We all have met Christians who know it all, and propound on it all. We know that such a tendency comes from insecurity. Still their stuffiness can become insufferable.

I have been told that humility comes from a root word "humus" that means dirt. Humor comes from the same root word. I think that there is a connection. A person doesn't have to be witty, but the ability to see something humorous in a dark and dirty situation can be a sign of health. As a pastor who deals with people who are sometimes in horrible situations, I know there is hope when a person starts looking at their own catastrophic situation, and finds some gallows humor somewhere. Last week a man in his seventies that I know found himself in jail, through his own fault. Being in "the tombs" in New York City, awaiting release, can be a horrifying experience. It could have destroyed his psyche. Instead, he found something to laugh about in the experience. He let out a big belly laugh. I knew he would be alright.

Sometimes the leader who lives the upside-down life just has to decide to "go with it," whatever the situation is. There is a power that comes when you have nothing left to hide. I remember a story a preacher told of a time when God was working in a group of people in a powerful way. The preacher was baptizing people out in the water, and as he baptized some people, more and more people began to come out of the crowd to be baptized too.

At one point, a very stylish, beautiful woman stepped into the water to profess Christ and be baptized. The preacher baptized her. As she went under the water, her wig floated off. She came up out of the water bald. She reached down, picked up the wet wig, lifted it above her head and shook it in contempt, as if it were a rat. "I'm free!" she shouted.

There is a humility that knows no humiliation, and it is one of the most powerful forces in leadership in my opinion. I watched it at work with a person who had a vision for sharing Christ in the South Bronx. The area he felt called to was the area that one survey had selected as the worst place to raise children in the city. I watched as he made the necessary contacts. I watched as people said that what he wanted to do wasn't productive. I watched as some treated him as if he were too young to handle the challenges of such a ministry in such an area. I watched as resources were hard to come by because the young man's ideas didn't fit the model that people felt was most result-driven. Another person could have taken all these circumstances as personal humiliations and quit with a pack of good reasons. Yet this person had a humility that knew no humiliation, and eventually his work began to thrive. Some of the very people who seemed dismissive at the beginning now want to publicize his success. You never know. He never treats them as if they did something wrong. The power of his refusal to nurse humiliation is a tangible force in his continued effectiveness.

The Snubbing of a President

Abraham Lincoln has a lot to teach us about humility. He had a lot of trouble with his commanding generals. George McClellan was an extremely accomplished general and beloved by his soldiers. His letters tell us that he didn't think much of Lincoln. One time Lincoln went over to talk to General Mc-Clellan with a member of his cabinet. McClellan was not there. Lincoln decided to wait for him in the parlor. When McClellan came home, he heard that the president was in his parlor, and he simply went on to bed. The president continued to wait. Finally he asked the servant how much longer he thought it would be before McClellan returned. He was informed that McClellan had returned and had gone to bed.

Lincoln's co-worker was astonished at the impudence of this snub to the President of the United States. Lincoln went home and didn't use the evening as a reason to censure the general. He once said he would hold McClellan's horse if a victory could be achieved.

Now many people would consider McClellan a somewhat self-serving and ineffectual general. The same people consider Lincoln to be one of the greatest leaders of all time. People's attempts to shame him didn't seem to be a motivator one way or another for Lincoln. In the end, McClellan did not win battles, and Lincoln took the bull by the horns and removed him. But it is clear that the general's removal was not based on his treatment of Lincoln.

This approach is nothing new. Jesus saw 12 men who were tired and dusty at the end of a day. The servant was the one who should be washing the camel and donkey manure from their feet. Jesus not only took up the towel of a servant and washed the disciples' feet, He even washed the feet of the one He knew would rat on Him and put Him in the place of deepest humiliation. This is a different kind of leader. We have forgotten His way.

An F in Life

When I read about the ancient world, I can't get over how odd it is that Christians chose the cross as the sign of their faith. The cross was the sign that you had failed in life, that you had gotten an F in living. If a member of your family had been crucified, and you were speaking to someone from the Roman world, you would avoid talking about it. One can sense, even a bit in the Book of Acts, how hard it was to communicate a faith-stance to a Gentile world in the Roman Empire, when the leader had not lived a long life nor died in battle bravely. It must have been hard to say that, yes, our leader taught us these things and then, well, He finally ended up being executed like a criminal by the Roman government. Yet Paul says he would only preach Christ crucified. Would you be able to take the thing about your life which society found most shameful and make it your brand?

Men and women all over the world put on a necklace with a little sign, large or small, to indicate what is most important to them. It is not a flower, it is not a jewel, it is not a moon, it is not a star—the kind of signs that other faiths and religions use. It is this sign of one of the greatest instruments of humiliation ever designed in human civilization. It is often made out of silver and gold, and sometimes has precious jewels embedded in it. Perhaps wearing it as beautiful jewelry helps us to handle the horrible thing it actually was. The original was not gold, and it had no precious jewels upon it—and it was the absolute opposite of pretty.

conclusion
The Upside-Down Savior

God delights in using failures.

sermon preached by David Wilkerson

Upside-Down Christians

Adoniram Judson became one of the most famous people in the nineteenth century, at least in some circles. But when you look at the facts of his life, he was an upside-down man. At times in his life, he was broken and had to learn the transcendent importance of following instead of leading. With so many years of frustration and discouragement, he had to learn sometimes to forget results. As we mentioned at the beginning, he was not all that stable at some points of his life. His plans didn't work out at all as he had thought—in fact, they crumbled. He had to deal with small groups of people, often one at a time, weary day after weary day, when he dreamed of affecting a nation.

Judson could have been a scholar, but he found himself bound up in filth with convicts. He was so immersed in the language and culture of his adopted country that as time progressed, he could hardly preach in English, his native tongue. He had lost touch with his American culture. He had a great lust to accomplish things, but for long periods in his life, dark periods, he could do nothing but stand there. Separated from his own national context, he was often treated as a pariah, a nobody. He had to embrace the fact that he wasn't what he could have been. If asked, I think he might have refused to write a book on leadership. He often wouldn't even share missionary stories when he finally returned for a bit to America. He thought there was Someone else who was far more important to preach about.

What if Peter, Simon Bar-Jonah, really was crucified upside down in Rome as the tradition maintains? What would he have thought about in those last hours, in the most extreme pain, looking at everyone's feet? Even his friends would have seemed upside down then. If the story we mentioned in the first of the book is true about how Peter died, I suppose he had that sense, that, even though he had messed so many things up in following Jesus, this time he had finally gotten things right.

God Wants a DNA Test

*O*ne of the greatest leaders I have ever seen used to be homeless. He works harder than anyone I know. He coordinates meals and clothing for people in trouble, and he never forgets to treat people like people. He is tireless in teaching people to stop making excuses that destroy their lives. He will teach a group or preach or mop a floor with equal intensity. He will sit waiting for others with an open Bible in his hand, and people crowd around him. Somehow he doesn't sound preachy.

There is a power that emanates from everything he does. He is not Superman. Sometimes people don't agree with what he does, but he does not let that paralyze him. Sometimes people are insensitive, but he does not let that stop him. Everything seems to go better when he is around. People laugh more and work together more.

He teaches firmly, but he always lets people know that he has been on the street and in crack houses and in mental institutions. He came back to God in an upside-down way, in a crack house, where people gathered around and talked about how they could do better. He says there is no sin, and he emphasizes strongly, *no sin* which is mentioned in the Bible which he has not done. He doesn't claim big educational degrees or job titles, yet if you watch closely, his influence is profound. He makes jokes about his previous time in mental institutions.

I have had the privilege of being his co-worker for the last ten years in New York City. Whenever I can, I sit in his Bible study, so that I can be under his teaching. He follows an upside-down Messiah whom we also claim to follow and to stand on His teachings. Yet we work hard to make Jesus' thoughts conform to what we think He should teach. In the long view, the further we go our own way in leadership, the further we eventually lose our way, even when we think we are achieving great goals, or fame, or producing lots of money, or some other great consequence. In the end, the results just won't stand up.

Every Wednesday a man stands outside our church and invites anyone who goes by to come in and have a meal with us. He does it because he remembers when he was homeless and needed something to eat and was angry at the world. At one time, he even threw garbage at a worker at our church when that person invited him to come and eat. This man doesn't feel as though he can get along with people, and yet he deals with all kinds of people, whether they are sober or drunk, kindly or angry.

He loves one-liners, such as "Jesus washed away my sins. Sorry about the ring around the tub." Or, "I am God's child. I think He wants a DNA test." When he shares in the Bible study, he shares from the heart about his own mental troubles and fears and inability to trust. He never sounds preachy and he always asks questions with the greatest humility. Things happen when he speaks. People pay attention. He doesn't think he is a leader, but I see that when he is not there, things just don't go right. He is one of my favorite unleaders. His weakness is what makes him so strong.

It's All About Timing

*I*n the letter to the Philippians, Paul talks about the power of the resurrection (3:10). The power of the resurrection is a challenging phrase. For Paul, it seems as though everything can become part of that resurrection power. If humiliation and crucifixion can be a part of this upside-down power, other things might be also. Boredom, lack of results, delay, failure, anything can be a part of this unheard-of power, culminating in that different kind of resurrection. And perhaps, as in the Bible sometimes, all those hard and difficult things can last for a really long time.

In the end, we are not in charge of checking whether the leaders of our churches and conferences are walking in this kind of resurrection power, or in some kind of surrogate, counterfeit power. But are we ourselves, as "unleaders," walking in this kind of power—power that includes the weak and difficult things of the world? Hudson Taylor is sometimes quoted as saying that Satan makes his servants strong and forceful, but God makes His servants weak, so that others can see God's power through them.

Many of us don't feel like leaders very often. We try to fit the conception of what a leader should be and we get disillusioned about ourselves and then we get exhausted. The Bible is filled with instructions for successful leaders, and the Bible is filled with insight for those of us who are discouraged. The ten principles cited in this book make suggestions to the rest of us, who are called to be leaders in our own sphere of influence, however large or small that sphere is. In the end, we really aren't capable of evaluating how important our small or large sphere really is. The sphere may be in our home, where we are a mother or father or uncle or aunt with few resources to lead the younger ones in the family. We may find ourselves out of our element in social groups, or in sports, or at our job, when a lot is depending on us. We may also feel out of our element in church, when we unknowingly contribute to our own sense of losing our way. Yet these periods of disorientation are good times for us to remember Adoniram Judson, mentioned at the beginning hanging upside down, watching everything he worked for look like such a failure. You never know, it may not be the end. If the basic leadership principles sound hollow to you, try some of the unleadership principles.

Christians talk about Good Friday. Well, it was certainly good for us. It wasn't so good for our leader. Good Friday stands for the worst things that can happen to us. And I mean the worst things, so take a moment and think of those things. If we stop to think about it, Good Friday is as if our worst nightmare came true. It is the time that the One through whom all of us were made came to us, His own, and we twisted everything upside down. And He let us, even though He had the power to stop us. That was the horror of Friday. In this context, Saturday represents that time of waiting, when we don't know what is going to come next. It is a time when all our hopes and dreams seem to have failed. The hardest thing about waiting is that sometimes you don't know how long you are going to have to wait. Saturdays can last a long time. People didn't really know when or even *if* the waiting would ever stop. Sunday stands for the newness and rebirth of things we never imagined could happen.

We know Fridays come in the world. We never know how long or short Saturdays will last. But if leaders, or any people in any time, only focus on Sunday, they've missed the boat.

There He Is Again

We are done. Abraham, Sarah, Moses, David, Paul of Tarsus, Adoniram Judson, Ann Judson, Hudson Taylor, Oswald Chambers, Biddy Chambers. We can talk about the rest, but in the end we always come back to Him. We circle around Him, that silent center of gravity, not even realizing it. He is the one who won't fit into any of our leadership categories, or neatly into any categories at all. He won't fit into any little book on leadership. He won't be a wheelbarrow for any of our ideas, no matter how hard we try. In His own time there were many more important and well-known leader-types, the Quiriniuses and Pontius Pilates of the world, governors and proconsuls of that period. But most of them we only remember now, even a little bit, because of Him.

We just can't figure Him out. He spoke with authority and thousands followed Him. He organized huge crowds into groups and then He fed them. His choice of people to mentor is structured and consistent, and yet somehow puzzling and unexpected. People had a parade in His honor, and yet abandoned Him quickly. He was focused and determined, and yet the places He went seemed so spontaneous, generating something like a moveable party, or perhaps a picnic.

He was called master or teacher, and yet He told the ones closest to Him not to mimic the leadership structures of the world. He liked to invert things. The greatest must be the servant; the first must be the last. He spent time with kids when He had a world to save, and it upset those around Him. His time management plan seemed a bit chaotic to some of His friends.

He talked about the righteousness of God, but spent time with precisely the wrong people, the hookers and the lepers and the ethically sleazy. By associating with them, He just seemed to be condoning all the wrong things. Some thought He was a bit off, telling people to choose the lowest place at the table and they will find their life when they lose it and all. He talked about severe justice, and yet stooped and washed the dirty toes of the very friend He knew had secretly betrayed Him.

Worst of all, He came to set people free, yet He knowingly allowed Himself to be trapped and snuffed out by the acknowledged oppressors, the enemies of His people and clearly the enemies of God. Sometimes, His leadership style seemed to mirror what looks like abysmal failure to us. With Him, the worst things, as well as the best things, sometimes happened.

We can't stop talking about Him. We have talked about Him for thousands of years, and we keep writing about Him, hundreds of millions of words, but we can't quite sort Him out. Even today those who ignore Him still quickly bring His name to their lips as a curse when things go wrong. Others say His name in honor all their lives, yet quietly drift further and further away from Him. He is still there. We can't quite adapt Him into any of our prevailing views. He is just so, well, so upside down.

We bring our questions to Him and eventually they lay limp and lifeless at His feet. If we look long enough, we realize it is the other way around. He is the one who is bringing His questions to us. What questions would He ask us as He walks through our places of power and financial influence today? What would He ask us in our proclamations of pride in governments and systems, as we choose comfort over courage, over and over again? How would He respond to our endless, mindless entertainment and media empires, the unending flow of trivial information that dominates our days? What would He say to the preoccupied, tunnel-visioned Wall Street investor, or to the addicted homeless man, lying about his needs, standing on the same block?

Or what about the structures that those who claim to be His followers have built, those works and ministries that have taken so much of our time that we have almost forgotten about Him? G. K. Chesterton was an English writer in the early twentieth century and a lover of paradox. He once said the task in life is to look at things familiar until they become unfamiliar again. Some are totally unaware of Him, while others of us have virtually ignored Him by making Him so, so familiar. What about the structures that were built to honor Him, but slowly, through time, become tainted with self-promotion, gossip, and well-intended goals of our own devices? What about our churches and our groups that have pretended that our goals are really His goals, and have become cynical if anyone raises the question to challenge our assertions?

It is relatively easy to take shots at other people, their leadership styles, their victories and their foibles. Anyone can do that. But He will not let us rest on our critique, and as we come to know Him, we begin to vaguely suspect that all our high-minded objectives and plans for others may not actually be His goals. For me, He is the oddest and truest leader. He always holds out a tiny speck of hope for us, in the midst of our mound of defeat and self-deceit. Like the emptiness of the tomb, He takes what is gone and then makes that vacant space the springboard for good news. He comes to us with His scars and His fresh-broken bread and asks us a question. Are we so sure that we are right side up?

appendix
Gallery of Unleaders
Mentioned in This Book

Note: I did not list every single person cited in this book in the Gallery of Unleaders. I only listed those who I felt had particular insights to offer in further reading. Some of the people listed below are people with very different views than my own. A few would not claim to be Christian. However, each of them made a connection with something in the book. If I didn't include someone about whom I wrote, I often listed the source of information within the book itself."

Abraham from Ur of the Chaldeans—How could the biblical Abraham have possibly conceived the extent of God's plan for him when he obeyed? We still are seeing the plan expand over 3,000 years later. Not that Abraham didn't try his own little plans at times, and had his own little "Ishmaels." But in spite of this, every one of God's promises came through. God blessed him and through him all nations blessed themselves, as some translations put it. Genesis 12—25 tells Abraham's story.

Sherwood Anderson—We used to study Sherwood Anderson in the American literature of the twentieth century. I have included Anderson in this gallery because he has such an ability to see the little person, the small detail, and the great dignity in lives that seem to others so drab. I mention his work under Principle #5 in talking about Herbert Hoover. His article on Herbert Hoover, "In Washington," in the *The Portable Sherwood Anderson* is so odd and upside down, it is wonderful.

Jim Cymbala—Pastor Jim has taught so many so much about weakness, being humble, and depending on God alone in prayer. He has reminded many to avoid slick techniques and entrepreneurial plans to accomplish God's purposes. He reminds those of us who have forgotten that it starts with prayer. We discuss him under Principle #4 because he had such a hard time getting started, and at first the attendance of his church in New York City was shrinking rather than expanding. I took my references from *Fresh Wind, Fresh Fire: What Happens When God's Spirit Invades the Heart of His People.*

Dietrich Bonhoeffer—Bonhoeffer was a brilliant German theologian and a man committed to the Word of God. He was executed by the Nazis at the end of World War II. The recent rather extensive biography of him by Eric Metaxas is called *Bonhoeffer: Pastor, Martyr, Prophet, Spy.* I took some of my thoughts from this book concerning the difficult choices he had to make as a pastor, as a responsible part of his society, as a person loyal to his country, and as a Christian loyal to the Word of God. Most of those thoughts about him are found in our section on embracing shame (Principle #10). For me, the only thing missing in the Metaxas biography is the excitement one feels as one reads Bonhoeffer's own books, such as *Life Together* or *The Cost of Discipleship.*

Jean-Pierre de Caussade — I love the words of this man, and I wish more people I know had read his little book *The Sacrament of the Present Moment.* Every unleader should read it, I think. He was a wonderful spiritual director in eighteenth-century France. De Caussade captures the joy of the obedience and surrender in the present moment to that presence of God's love. He helps us think of the vastness of God's purposes and how we are simply a tool in His hands, content to do anything, or nothing. The vast web of connections of cause and effect may bless people in times and spaces that we cannot imagine. It is a tribute to the impact of his words to learn that the Sisters at Nancy preserved his words from his talks to them and passed them from person to person, for over a hundred years, before they were published.

Gertrude "Biddy" Chambers — We quote Oswald Chambers in sermons, but Biddy made it happen. As Oswald's wife, she did all the work of editing and compiling his works, and much of the transcribing to begin with. Without her, Chambers' work would have been remembered by the generation that heard him preach and teach, and that would have been all. The end of McCasland's book, mentioned in Oswald's entry, gives a flavor of Biddy's life — she was a quiet unleader who did so much. After Oswald's death in 1917, she spent her remaining 30 years editing and publishing his works.

Oswald Chambers — Chambers is, for me, the poster child of the unleader. He made obscure and puzzling career choices in terms of education and positions. He was a wonderful Scottish preacher and lecturer. He died, worn and depleted in Egypt, at the age of 43. Not many would have foreseen the influence then that he would have. In his devotional book, *My Utmost for His Highest*, so many of our cherished religious thoughts are turned upside down by his biblical insight. I took my thoughts and quotes by him from the wonderful biography of him by David McCasland, called *Oswald Chambers: Abandoned to God*. I referred mostly to Chambers because he talks so much about obedience to God in antithesis to our earthly plans. However, he is so insightful as the talks about the uncertainty and lack of ability the unleader might feel. Here is a part of a note he left on the pillow of his wife Biddy. She, to me, is one of the true heroes of Oswald's story: "The feeling of futility and incompetence is not a bad one because it comes near His beatitude—Poverty in brain and body and heart is blessed if it will drive us on to His fathomless resources."

David son of Jesse—After the biblical David was anointed to be king, he knew what it was like to be a fugitive. He understood what it meant to sleep in a cave. He understood what it was like to act like a homeless mental case in order not to be killed by his enemies. As we discuss under Principle #4, David knew what it was like to think small, to go from great victories and royal success to offering up his broken and contrite heart. It was the only way. You can read the honest, gripping story of his life in First and Second Samuel. You can read the lyrics to his songs in Psalms.

Elisha son of Shaphat—Elisha is a wonderful example of an unleader in the Bible because for years he lived in the shadow of a very magnetic, dramatic prophet, Elijah. Yet as we read the stories about Elisha, it is as though God works through him in a different way, because Elisha is such a different person. He has a quiet style and he doesn't seem to try to imitate his predecessor, though he asked for a double portion of his spirit. Elisha becomes the master of the undramatic moment, as Naaman the Syrian general brings his entire entourage to Elisha's little house, and Elisha simply sends his servant out to tell him to wash seven times in the Jordan River. Naaman is incensed that Elisha doesn't do anything dramatic, and feels as though the rivers in his country are so much grander than the waters of Israel. When Naaman finally obeys, he is wonderfully healed. The disarming stories of Elisha are found in 1 and 2 Kings. Elisha is mentioned in Principle #4 because he often seems to follow "the little way."

Charles de Foucauld — I have often come across this story of the French Catholic priest in Algeria who saw himself as the advance agent for a community of Little Brothers. But no followers ever came before his death. In the chapter on thinking small (Principle #4), I quoted from his letter to a friend concerning his time in the desert in Algeria. I have mostly gotten information from the summaries of his life on the internet.

Mohandas K. Gandhi — In the park close to my apartment in New York City, there is a massive statue of George Washington on a horse. Further back, is a huge statue of Abraham Lincoln. In one small corner of the park, a thin little statue of a man with a walking stick stands. It is Gandhi. Gandhi did not consider himself a Christian, but he followed many of Jesus' commandments. We discuss him in Principle #8, because he confined his actions in an ethical box, so to speak. He refused to lie. He refused to use violence even when it seemed so necessary. He refused to treat people as enemies regardless of the brutality he experienced. He was assassinated before he saw the dream of an independent India fulfilled. The little biography called *Gandhi: His Life and Message for the World* by Louis Fischer is a great introduction to him. Gandhi's own writing, *An Autobiography: The Story of My Experiments with Truth* is longer, but it is a classic.

Gideon son of Joash — We just had to include Gideon in our gallery. In the Bible, he seems like such a scaredy cat and he asks the angel a lot of obnoxious, doubting questions. Eventually God limits the number of people following him to one percent of what originally followed him. But when God uses that one percent, all the circumstances seem to change (Judges 6–8).

Robert Greenleaf — A generation ago, Greenleaf challenged the categories that the American business world and others held concerning leadership. Of course, his challenge wasn't really something new. It was a hearkening back to the model of Jesus and others. *Servant Leadership* is one of his strong books on the subject. I consider some of his thoughts foundational to what we talk about for unleaders.

Jesus of Nazareth — He refuses to be categorized. He wrote no books.

Clarence Jordan — Jordan was a Southern Baptist who soaked himself in the Greek New Testament and shared a vision for a new kind of racially integrated community. This vision was pretty tough in Georgia in the 1950s. Jordan watched his community dwindle at the end of his life. Clarence and his wife Florence were tired and disappointed at the way the experiment in community turned out. However, they could little imagine the rebirth and directions that came from it eventually. Some of the story can be found in *The Cotton Patch Evidence: The Story of Clarence Jordan and the Koinonia Farm Experiment* by Dallas Lee. A couple of the stories I mention are from memory from 30 years ago.

Adoniram Judson — Adoniram and his wife, Ann, were America's first missionaries sent overseas. Reading Rosalie Hall Hunt's *Bless God and Take Courage: The Judson History and Legacy* helped me begin to think about writing this book. Judson has one of the most amazing conversion stories (you'll have to read about it in his biography).

His willingness to endure phenomenal discouragement and suffering and his passionate scholarship in service of missions became an inspiration to me. He helped change my conception of a leader. Each of his three wives is a distinctive hero also — Ann, Sarah, and Emily. I am grateful for some insights in conversation with his biographer, Rosalie Hunt. In telling Judson's story, I also used *The Life of Adoniram Judson* by his son, Edward Judson, and *Adoniram Judson: Missionary to Burma* by Faith Coxe Bailey.

Ann Judson — She deserves special note. Her work to help her husband, Adoniram Judson, while he was imprisoned hanging upside down, is a tribute to her unrelenting ingenuity. She described herself at this time as "a solitary, unprotected female" in a foreign country that was more and more hostile to her presence, due to the war between Burma and Britain. She was devoted to her husband at the expense of her own welfare. Rosalie Hunt's book, mentioned above, gives a remarkable portrait of Ann's work before her death. I think that Ann Judson was an astonishing woman.

Edward Judson — One of the great surprises in reading about the missionary Adoniram Judson was finding out more about his son, Edward Judson. His remarkable ministry took place in my own neighborhood in Lower Manhattan. His Address on the Judson Centennial in 1914 is one of the most profound sermons I have ever read. I wish more people would read it. I think he really understood a bit more about what God was doing with his father, and how God works in what I call His unleaders. Rosalie Hunt's book, mentioned above, has a section on Edward.

Brother Lawrence — Nicholas Herman, or Brother Lawrence, entered a monastery in the seventeenth century and spent the next 30 years as a cook. People were drawn to him and his quiet ways — who would have anticipated the influence this lame, awkward, low-skilled person would have? He is a wonderful unleader. I speak of him in Principle #7 on doing nothing. Brother Lawrence is incisive in speaking of how addicted we get to activities for God. We could have placed him in the section on thinking small. Here is a quote from the wonderful book *The Practice of the Presence of God*: "That we ought not to be weary in doing little things for the love of God, who regards not the greatness of the work, but the love with which it is performed."

Abraham Lincoln — To me, Lincoln is one of the greatest leaders and *unleaders* of all time. He is a puzzle. He was the only president that never joined a church, yet his later speeches are laced with more biblical references than practically any other president. Many preachers will cite the string of failures that Lincoln encountered on his path to the presidency. I was most impressed by Lincoln's strong sense of direction combined with his acknowledgment that we are subject to a purpose of God, which we cannot truly fathom. Doris Kearns Goodwin's *Team of Rivals: The Political Genius of Abraham Lincoln* is truly an inspiring historical book, and I took my references to Lincoln concerning his political decisions from it.

Martin Luther — Luther, the reformer of the sixteenth century, had some attributes of an unleader. As Luther tells the story long afterwards, the study of one word in the Greek from Romans opened up the windows of revelation for him and eventually changed the face of Europe. That revelation also helped start the Reformation with the return to the Bible itself as our source of faith. Just one word in Greek. That should encourage the detail-loving scholars among us. More importantly for unleaders, Luther saw the deep biblical truths as opposites, paradoxes. You couldn't live without the opposites. He did not preach at a megachurch. He lived in a town with a population of 2,000 and worked with the church there. He was so frustrated with the villagers' lack of spiritual growth after the insights of the Reformation that he even quit preaching for a while. Even great Reformation leaders had their challenges. I am grateful to

The Cambridge Companion to Martin Luther, edited by Donald McKim, and *Martin Luther: Selections from His Writings*, edited by John Dillenberger, and *Martin Luther's Theology: Its Historical and Systematic Development*, by Bernhard Lohse.

George MacDonald — MacDonald was a Scottish minister and author of the nineteenth century. His writings had a profound influence on later Christian writers, such as C. S. Lewis. One small church where he served as pastor didn't like his views. They cut his salary in half. He continued to preach there but finally had to resign. He did have a sense of the inverted nature of many of God's ways. Anyone who could say, "There is no escaping God but by running into His arms," is close to an unleader's view. I discuss his understanding of the Lord coming down the "secret stair" in life under Principle #3. This idea has helped me immeasurably in my prayer life. I appreciate *Getting to Know Jesus*, edited by Warner A. Hutchinson, for the thought-provoking sermons from MacDonald's life.

Moses from Egypt — Moses is in the gallery because his career trajectory is so unusual. It is almost inverted. He started strong, and then had 40 years in the desert as a shepherd, before he led the people. During those 40 years, he didn't seem to be making the greatest vocational choices. You never know. Exodus tells a lot of his story. It continues through Deuteronomy.

George Muller — Muller had a heart for children with no parents, and he had such a heart for obedience to God. He quietly went about his business for God without asking any person on earth for anything. *The Autobiography of George Muller* is remarkable for many reasons, but I mentioned him in the chapter on forgetting results (Principle #2) because of the deliberate way he records his waiting on God before proceeding, so different from the model of the bold, quick, decisive leader.

Noah — My New Yorker son says that Noah building an ark in that particular area is like a guy with an apartment in Manhattan building a lawn mower. It just didn't make sense. For me, the important thing about Noah is that he walked with God. In the context of the story, God's plan for him seemed bizarre and absurd, and yet the value of the real results were practically inestimable. His story is found in Genesis 5–10.

The Old Fellow (English translation of Lao Tzu) — Lao Tzu lived in China centuries before Christ. One might wonder why Lao Tzu would be in the list of evangelical Christians, but in terms of the topic of the unleader, the Old Fellow has a lot to say that sounds like Jesus. I lived next to a Taoist temple when I lived in Hong Kong, and I have seen firsthand how distant the practitioners have become from those original writings. However, I think Jesus Himself might say that the Old Fellow was not far from the kingdom of God in some of the things he said about leadership. Huston Smith in the classic *The Religions of Man* gives a good summary of some of the teachings.

Paul of Tarsus — We had to include him in this list. For me, the key unleadership manual in Paul's work is Second Corinthians. He was accused of not having an influential presence and of not being a good speaker. In the Corinthian church, he seemed to be up against the ropes. Remarkably, Paul ends up bragging about his weakness, using it almost as a badge, and proclaiming that when he is weak, then he is strong. What an unleader.

Peter son of John (Simon Bar-Jonah) — In my mother's old Bible, we found this written next to Peter's refusal to have his feet washed in John 13: "Jesus is willing to wash your feet if you will take them out of your mouth." Peter got a lot of things wrong, but still Jesus appointed him as leader. The reference to the tradition that Peter was crucified upside down comes from a document later than the New

Testament—*The Acts of Peter* (second century A.D.). Here is more of what Peter said in that text: "Unless ye make the things of the right hand as those of the left, and those of the left as those of the right, and those that are above as those below, and those that are behind as those that are before, ye shall not have knowledge of the kingdom." This sounds like an inverted, upside-down unleader to me.

Franklin D. Roosevelt—Historians speculate on what would have happened if Roosevelt hadn't contracted polio. Would he have run for president at the wrong time? Would he have ever become president? Would he have been the leader he was if he hadn't worked so hard to overcome his own difficulties? Would he have ever been able to say with such conviction, "There is nothing to fear but fear itself"? I like to look at his portrait on the dime and think about how instrumental he was in the starting of the March of Dimes, and in helping protect so many others from polio. Would that have happened, if he hadn't had his own upside-down experiences? The things I mention under Principle #5 about Roosevelt are common knowledge. I cried a bit when I visited his museum at Hyde Park.

Albert Schweitzer—Schweitzer continues to be for me one of the most remarkable personalities of the twentieth century, though he is not mentioned much in contemporary culture. Although his theological convictions reflect the European premises of the nineteenth and early twentieth century and are quite different from my own, Schweitzer is a great example of an unleader's trajectory. Leaving his extremely successful careers to go to the Congo was incomprehensible to most at the time. When people asked why he did it, he would simply say, "Because my master told me to." The quote from the section on becoming a nobody (Principle #9) is from his work, *Out of My Life and Thought.* Another extensive but excellent book is *Albert Schweitzer: A Biography* by James Brabazon. I cannot resist including this lengthier quote from the biography, taken from a sermon Schweitzer preached when he was 30. It not only expands on the unleadership notion of being small, but also shows how the entire environment changes when this direction is taken:

> To content oneself with becoming small, that is the only salvation and liberation. To work in the world as such, asking nothing of it, or of men, not even recognition, that is true happiness. . . . There are things which one cannot do without Jesus. Without Him one cannot attain to that higher innocence — unless we look to Him in the disappointments of life, and seek in Him the strength to be childlike and small in that higher sense. Whoever has gone through the world of smallness has left the empire of this world to enter into the kingdom of God. He has gone over the border as one goes over the border in a dark forest — without taking note of it. The way remains the same, the surrounding things the same, and only gradually does he realize that whilst everything is familiar it is different, that life is the same and yet not the same because of the clarity which lights up in him, and because of the peace and strength which have taken possession of him because he is small and has finished with himself.

Nassim Nicholas Taleb — Taleb might seem a strange person to be in the gallery of unleaders. He is a former financial trader and professor and is interested in issues related to uncertainty and probability. I include him because he often has something very original to say about leaders. He has helped me see that from some perspectives, humans are very ill-equipped to evaluate whether someone is a successful leader or not. We simply don't have enough information. The first example from his work concerning our inability to evaluate good leadership is from *The Black Swan: The Impact of the Highly Improbable*. The second example I use about leaders who have gained by chance in the same section is taken from *Fooled by Randomness: The Hidden Role of Chance in Life and in the Markets*.

Hudson Taylor — I have heard people quote Taylor as saying, "It is not great faith in God we need, but faith in a great God." He is an example of someone who seemed to others like a nobody, but who helped people see the greatness of God. It is hard to estimate the effect of his missionary outreach to China in the nineteenth century. I took my story concerning Taylor from *J. Hudson Taylor: A Man in Christ* by Roger Steer.

Therese of Lisieux — Therese did not live a long life in France in the nineteenth century, but she was an unleader by talking about the Little Way. She helped people understand that small things can be done in great love. She helped Christians, and people in general, see the world in a different way. "God cares nothing for the deed itself, but He cares greatly about the most trivial act if it is done to please Him and to show that we love Him." This quote comes from *Saint Therese, the Little Flower* by John Beevers. Richard Foster also writes movingly about her in *Prayer: Finding the Heart's True Home.* I quote Therese briefly in the chapter on thinking small (Principle #4). I found the quote on an ancient index card and don't know its source.

J. R. R. Tolkien — I include the English writer Tolkien because he had such a strong sense in *The Lord of the Rings* of the fact that the small commonplace person may be the one to turn the tide in the huge stage of affairs. All the great warriors and kings, in the end, place their hope in Frodo, the little halfling, and his journey to do the unexpected in the dark land of Mordor. Tolkien was suspicious of leaders, for leadership itself can become deceiving. In *The Letters of J. R. R. Tolkien*, he writes to his son that "the most improper job of any man . . . is bossing other men. Not one in a million is fit for it, and least of all those who seek the opportunity."

Taylor Field is the pastor of a church that rarely has more than 100 people on Sunday. He has been in the same location for more than 25 years. Much of that time, the ministry worked out of a storefront. He often works during the week with people society would label as underachievers. He doesn't know many influential people. He has not advanced in his career nor moved his location. None of his books have made the *New York Times* best-seller list. Not even close. He seldom speaks at conferences around the country and, when he does, the groups are small. He works with Graffiti Community Ministries in the Lower East Side in New York City.

Graffiti Community Ministry

started in a storefront more than 35 years ago. Now it works to express God's love in tangible ways for thousands each year. It has also started Graffiti 2 in the South Bronx, and Graffiti 3 in Brooklyn, as well as fostering and supporting almost 20 new churches while acting as mother church, aunt church, or grandmother church. It partners with a number of other ministries in New York City in a commitment to do the small thing to serve the unserved. For more information, contact Graffiti Community Ministry at 205 E. 7th Street, New York, NY 10009, (212) 473-0044, or go to graffitichurch.org.

Use the QR reader on your
smartphone to visit us online at
www.newhopedigital.com

If you've been blessed by this book, we would like to hear your story. The publisher and author welcome your comments and suggestions at: newhopereader@wmu.org.

Leadership Resources

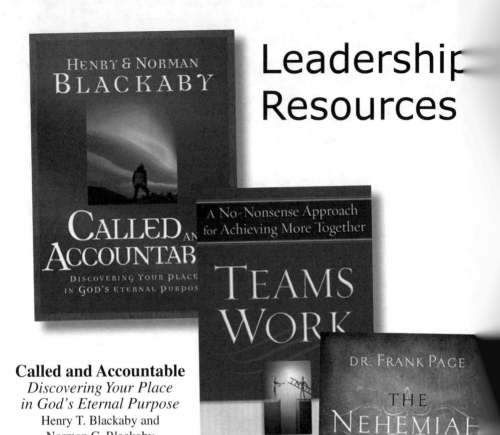

Called and Accountable
Discovering Your Place
in God's Eternal Purpose
Henry T. Blackaby and
Norman C. Blackaby
ISBN-13: 978-1-59669-047-9
N064153 • $19.99

TeamsWork
A No-Nonsense Approach
for Achieving More Together
Joyce A. Mitchell
ISBN-13: 978-1-59669-211-4
N084136 • $12.99

Available in bookstores everywhere.
For information about these books
or any New Hope product,
visit newhopedigital.com.

The Nehemiah Factor
16 Characteristics
of a Missional Leader
Dr. Frank S. Page
ISBN-13: 978-1-59669-223-7
N084146 • $14.99